The Accrington

Pals

A Play

^n or before

Peter Whelan

Samuel French – London
New York – Sydney – Toronto – Hollywood

The Accrington Pals was first presented by the Royal Shakespeare Company at the Warehouse, London, on 10 April 1981, with the following cast:

MAY, a stallholder, late twenties or older	Janet Dale
TOM, an apprentice, nineteen	Nicholas Gecks
RALPH, a clerk, nineteen or so	Peter Chelsom
EVA, a millgirl, the same age as RALPH	Trudie Styler
SARAH, a married mill worker, mid-twenties	Sharon Bower
BERTHA, a millgirl, eighteen	Hilary Townley
ANNIE, a housewife, late thirties	Brenda Fricker
ARTHUR, her husband, of similar age	Andrew Jarvis
REGGIE, her son, fourteen/fifteen	Vincent Hall
C.S.M. RIVERS, a regular soldier, thirties/forties	Bob Peck

Directed by Bill Alexander
Designed by Kit Surrey
Lighting by Michael Calf
Sound by John A. Leonard
Music arranged by Peter Washtell

Setting

Two main stage areas: MAY's street corner greengrocery stall in Accrington and the kitchen of her two-up-two-down terraced house nearby.

The stall, when closed, serves as a backdrop to the military scenes at camp in England, or on the Western front.

The variations on this general scheme are the recruiting office in Act One and SARAH's backyard in Act Two.

Minimal settings are intended, as there is a great deal of visual overlap between scenes, created by lighting changes.

The action takes place between autumn 1914 and July 1916. The background is reality. The 'Accrington Pals' batallion of Kitchener's New Army was raised and destroyed as described in the play.

Otherwise all the characters in the play, and the events of their lives, are entirely fictitious.

Note on the music

My Drink is Water Bright (Act One, Scene One) used a hymn tune called *Merry Dick*, but it goes quite well to *Old Soldiers Never Die*.

Boys Brigade March

Author's Preface

As a child, I was fascinated by a fuzzy snapshot of my mother taken in the first world war. It was the time she volunteered as a female lumberjack . . . or was it 'lady forester'? I could hardly credit it. A less likely feller of trees than my mother I couldn't imagine, yet there she was, leaning in a very posed, dewy-eyed Edwardian fashion on the upturned handle of a full blooded woodsman's axe, somewhere in the home counties . . . a million miles from the Salford street she grew up in (an exact twin of Coronation Street, now bulldozed away for ever).

I suppose what I couldn't believe was that my mother as I knew her then . . . stout, middle-aged and living entirely for her family . . . had ever experienced such release. Doors had once been opened and then slammed shut, as they had been for millions of young women in that war. And through the doors they had glimpsed tantalising freedoms as well as unimaginable horrors.

So I think I'd always wanted to write something about working-class women in the Great War. Then, maybe nine or ten years ago, I read Martin Middlebrook's *The First Day On The Somme,* a pulverising account of Britain's awakening to machine-age violence.

One short paragraph stayed in my mind. It concerned the town of Accrington, Lancashire which had raised its own batallion, 'The Accrington Pals', for Kitchener's New Army. After the Somme battle, Middlebrook tells us how the towns-people, driven desperate by rumours of disaster and angered by ludicrously optimistic reports in the press, surrounded the Mayor's house to demand the truth.

For me this was like looking through a pin-hole into the past and finding a whole vista of humanity revealed in a very unexpected way. These mothers, wives, daughters and lovers of the Pals didn't knuckle under sheepishly to authority in the way I had supposed. They realised perfectly well that there was an 'us and them' situation with regard to war information. Soldiers and sailors on leave contradicted the official hand-outs. Those women resented government secrecy then as we do today — and suspected, as we do, that much of it was a cover-up for blundering at the top.

Now I had the background for a play but not the foreground. That came to me two years ago while sitting in The Other Place during breaks in rehearsals of *Captain Swing*. There were a lot of sounds of clogs on bare boards in that play and the sounds took me back to a Lowry-like picture of Salford as I dimly recalled it from childhood, when visiting my uncles and aunts.

I began to evolve the story of a clash-cum-love relationship between a strong-minded, rugged individualist woman and a dreamy, Utopian idealist young man. Such a relationship was very much in keeping with those early years of the century when there were two clear ways that working people could see of improving their lot. One was the individualistic route — get yourself a little corner shop etc. The other was through collectivism and trade unionism. And since my family at that time contained both shopkeepers and "dreamy" socialists, it held a vivid basic attraction for me. I was now dealing not with history but with the edge of living memory. Details of my family folk-lore came to me in a rush.

One evening at a crowded pub in Stratford I grabbed the unsuspecting parents of one of the actors and poured out the whole story to them with frequent stops for adjustments and digressions. I hope I bought them a drink afterwards. So background and foreground had now come together in that explosive way that sustains a writer through the actual process of putting the play down on paper.

In choosing a self-confessed individualist for my main character, I hope I am being conscious, without being artificially conscious, of contemporary parallels. It seems like the wheel turning full circle that the Samuel Smiles self-help mentality is back in the political arena.

Older working-class generations may remember how the rows between paddle-your-own-canoe individualists and socialist-inclined trade unionists split families down the middle. Now the wedge is being driven in again. And maybe it's one of the basic contradictions that split personalities, let alone families. How much am I for others? How much am I for myself? Twenty years ago I might have said that the reconciliation of this con-tradiction was the answer to the Socratic question: how shall we live? But today it takes on a global urgency as we face the question: how shall we survive?

We are all crossing no-man's land now.

Peter Whelan

ACT ONE

Scene One

The market stall, closed up; a winter morning.
    TOM HACKFORD *pulls on a hand cart of green groceries. He unties the stall covers, lights the lamp and begins to transfer the produce to the stall. He wears a rain cape under which we can see his army trousers, puttees and army boots.*
    MAY HASSAL *enters, a shawl over her head, the iron scales in one hand, an enamel jug of tea in the other. She had a grudge against him and he knows it.*

MAY. So. You got up.

TOM. As per.

MAY. You look like a corpse.

TOM. It's cold enough.

MAY. I wasn't talking about the cold. Shove those baskets back.

    As he does so she places the scales on the stall.

TOM. It's laying off a bit. Was raining stair rods at quarter to five.

MAY. I saw.

TOM. Oh?

MAY. I could see through the window. I was awake listening for you getting out in case you weren't capable.

TOM. I'm all right.

    He begins to flick and stamp his boot.

MAY. You'll injure your brains.

TOM. Dratted things let water in.

MAY. They weren't issued for working.

TOM. They'll have to stand up to worse than this on manoeuvres.

MAY (*pouring tea into mugs*): That's a word you love isn't it?

TOM. What?

MAY. Manoeuvres. (*She hands him a mug.*) Stir that or you won't taste the sugar.

TOM. When it comes down to doing anything properly, they've got no idea. Someone decides that because a boot's for marching then it must have a thick sole. They don't think about the weight of the sole pulling down on the uppers. They don't consider the nature of the material. If the sole was three-quarters as thick . . . or even half . . . so it could flex as you marched it would actually wear longer. But if you said that they wouldn't understand. It's the same with the way they run everything. They're boneheads. They don't comprehend.

MAY. We'll have a ha'penny on carrots.

TOM *gives a disapproving look.*

A ha'penny. I don't make the shortages. They're a penny a pound on at the Co-op.

TOM *takes the blackboard and re-chalks the price.* MAY *regards him for a while.*

You think I'm going to say nothing don't you?

TOM. About what?

MAY. When it comes down to it . . . at the end . . . you're on your own. Oh Tom, whatever did you think you were doing last night?

TOM. How d'you mean?

MAY. You and Ralph and the rest, making all that noise outside the house at gone midnight.

TOM. We thought you'd still be up.

MAY. What's the difference whether I was up or down? You

woke every family in the street.

TOM. Just a bit of a send-off. Some of them were with us.

MAY. Who were?

TOM. Neighbours.

MAY. Then I'm even more ashamed. You've never seen me cry have you?

TOM *shakes his head.*

Well, I came close to it last night.

TOM. You could have come along.

MAY. I wouldn't waste my existence. Stinking pipes, stale beer and smutty songs. No sir, not me. You can think it's a celebration, marching off to camp. Well march away! After what I heard you shout last night I'm glad to see you go.

TOM. What?

MAY. I heard you from the bedroom. 'I'm free of her!' I heard you distinctly, top of your voice. 'I'm free of her!' It was you. My father put a roof over your head when you came here from Salford. We gave you work so you'd have pocket money. And when he died I could have said: I'm sorry Tom, you'll have to leave. We can't share the same house. But I didn't. I could see you couldn't afford to. I let you stay on and I made it clear in every way you were under no obligation. And now I see you've treated it as some form of bondage. 'I'm free of her!'

TOM. I didn't say that.

MAY. You did. Shouted it so everyone could hear. You slighted me.

TOM. I didn't say 'free of *her*'. I said 'free of *here*'.

MAY. Oh don't demean yourself.

TOM. Free of here . . . of this place . . . of this town.

MAY. Of this town?

TOM. That's what I meant.

MAY. But you've always preferred Accrington to Salford.

TOM. Aye. But that's not saying much is it?

MAY. You twister! (*Laughs.*) You almighty twister!

TOM. There's no twisting in it.

MAY. You may be a dreamer. You may go on about improving the mind and your world's famous thinkers . . . but you're a twister. I won't say another word. March away! If you can. I heard you fall down three times on the stairs last night.

TOM. I'll have to sign the pledge again.

MAY. You? They'll have drummed you out of the Band of Hope for good and all!

TOM (*sings*): 'My drink is water bright . . . water bright . . . water bright'.

MAY. Where's the plums?

TOM. Oh . . . aye . . . they hadn't got none.

MAY. They had.

TOM. They hadn't. The waggoner's gone to France in the artillery. The old man that's taken over does it all at a snail's pace apparently . . . he hadn't shown up.

MAY. They hide them! If there's a shortage they'll tell you all sorts! You have to ferret and burrow and not take 'no'. All the result of that is they'll have plums on the market stalls and we'll have none in Waterloo Street and you know how the girls like a plum on their way to work. But you're out of it aren't you? Dreamer!

TOM. What's it to do with dreaming?

MAY. Oh you're so obstinate and you know perfectly well. Dreaming is not making your own decisions but letting others make them for you. There are some kinds of men that are forever making themselves prey for others . . . falling in . . . getting swept along. And they're so overjoyed when they're welcomed in by their new cronies . . . 'Young Tom! Move along for young Tom . . . what'll you drink Tom? I don't want to see you like that, throwing all away for a little bit of buttering up. Cos all they want to see is you failing. They love failure. Delight in it. They see someone like you who has the ability to get on and they're just waiting to see you stumble, slip back and be as they are. In the end it's you . . . yourself. We don't create the rules of life. They're there.

TOM. Then it depends which way you read them.

A silence.
Presently we hear the knocker-up approaching, tapping on the windows with a pole to wake the mill girls.

ARTHUR (*off*): Rise and shine Elsie James . . . quarter to six.

ARTHUR BOGGIS enters. He is in uniform with a gas cape. He taps at a window.

ARTHUR. Are you there Mrs Bloor and Brenda? Quarter to six. Rise and shine.

MAY. What are you doing, knocking up, Arthur?

ARTHUR. Morning May . . . Tom. Jack's got the siatica and as I was to be up early for the great day I said I'd do this end of the street while his son does the other.

MAY. So it's you that's ruined the weather.

ARTHUR. It's God's weather.

MAY. Ah, but does he get wet in it?

ARTHUR. A question I've never asked.

TOM. Well look! It's clearing up. Is that a sign?

ARTHUR. It can be if you want it to be. But why look for signs when the true destination is always before you? We are all of us on the threshold of the celestial city if we have hearts to see with. (*He taps another window.*) Rise and shine Mary . . . (*He pauses looking at his watch.*) Thirteen minutes to six.

He goes.

MAY. Pull the pears to the front seeing there's no plums . . .

REGGIE BOGGIS enters furtively.

What are you up to Reggie?

REGGIE. Was that me father?

MAY. You know it was.

REGGIE. Has Mother been out?

MAY. Any minute. Why?

REGGIE. Haven't been home.

TOM. All night?

MAY. She'll paddle you!

REGGIE. I know.

TOM. Make yourself scarce.

MAY. Don't interfere.

REGGIE. I was at the Pals sing-song wasn't I Mr Hackford?

> MAY *gives* TOM *a look.*

TOM. I didn't see him.

MAY. Wait round the corner. I don't want her paddling you here.

> *As* REGGIE *goes he almost collides with* RALPH *who is in uniform and carrying a suitcase.*

RALPH. Go get your bugle Reggie! Chorley's up and marching. Blackburn's forming fours!

> (*Aside to* TOM:) What she say? Is it all right?

> *Before* TOM *can answer* MAY *rounds on* RALPH.

MAY. You! Bawling and caterwauling last night spoiling people's sleep.

RALPH. England shake off your downy slumbers. Men of Lancashire all parts of the Empire are responding nobly to the call. Shall Accrington and district be behind?

> (*In a quick aside to* TOM:) Shall they arseholes!

> EVA MASON *has entered, carrying her belongings in an old carpet bag. She stands apart shyly.* RALPH *introduces her as though* MAY *should know her.* TOM *looks guilty.*

> May . . . this is Eva Mason. Eva . . . May Hassal.

MAY. How d'you do?

EVA. How d'you do?

RALPH. A young lady in a million or any number you care to name. She can write copperplate as good as him and does sums up to long division. And strong? She's a female Eugene Sandow.

EVA. He does his best to embarrass me.

MAY. It's nice to meet you. I'm sorry you catch us at our busy time with the world about to descend on us.

RALPH. Tom . . . have you asked her?

TOM. Not in full. You see . . . with me going off to Caernarvon with the Pals . . . the idea was that she'd like to take over my early turn on the stall . . . from tomorrow.

MAY. Oh.

EVA. She doesn't know!

RALPH. It's not just that Tom. (*To* MAY:) We thought he'd have told you. He said he had. We thought she could have his room. She's come from t'other side of Clayton-le-Moors on the strength of that.

EVA. I don't know where to put myself. I thought it was settled.

TOM. I'm sorry.

MAY. You'll waste your life being sorry.

EVA. This isn't fair to you Miss Hassal . . .

MAY. Nor to you. (*To* TOM:) Dolly day-dream. Couldn't you speak?

RALPH. She's worked on farms on the poultry and the milking. She's used to getting up early.

MAY. Has she? Well she doesn't want to be standing out here with her cases. Take Miss Mason's things and put them in the scullery, Tom.

RALPH. There you are!

MAY. And be quick. She can have your room tonight at any rate. There's no reason it should go empty.

TOM takes the bags and goes off to the house. MAY sets up her scales and cash box.

RALPH. What did I say? Straight as a die May Hassal.

MAY. And this is the man who calls me a tartar.

RALPH. Now! Only once.

MAY. I am a bit of a tartar, you'll find. You have to be round here. You have to breathe fire.

EVA. It shouldn't be thrust on you like this. I'm very sorry for it.

MAY. No . . . I'd be glad of your help. Watch how it goes and try a turn tomorrow. Then you can see.

EVA. I've always wanted to get work down here. I tried for the mills but there's so many laid off.

MAY. Don't I know. I see it in my takings.

RALPH. Where's the work they should be getting making khaki for Kitchener's New Army? Hambledon, Helene, Broad Oak, Fountain, Paxton and Victoria . . . all shut down for repairs. Repairs? It's nothing but a bloody lock-out.

MAY. Don't pose as the worker's friend, Ralph. As a clerk you should be above such things. (*She knows how to tease him.*)

RALPH. Should I? I'm kissing that goodbye, thank God! I'll not push a pen anymore.

Enter TOM.

Come on Tom. Let's get on parade.

TOM. I'll do my turn.

RALPH. Your last clog chorus.

EVA. Clog chorus?

RALPH. Yes . . . you don't get that on the farm! You don't know what we're talking about do you?

He gives her a rub on the backside.

MAY. Take your hand from there please.

RALPH. And keep your mind on the fruit. I'll have a couple of pears.

Through this we hear the sound of street doors slamming, clogs clattering on stone cobbles and women calling out to each other.

TOM *weighs two pears for* RALPH.

VOICES. Elsie! Get yourself down here! Wait on me Mary! If you're not down in one minute . . . Mary don't go. You'll be late for Christmas!

MAY (*to* EVA): Watch Tom on the weighing out. Has to be done to a farthing and they always try to get the benefit if you're over.

RALPH *holds up the two pears suggestively.*

RALPH. Oh lovely! How perfect in form. How goodly to behold!

He gives one to EVA. ANNIE BOGGIS *comes on.*

ANNIE. Reggie! Come here!

MAY. Oh not this morning!

ANNIE. Come here at once!

REGGIE *emerges with a half grin of resignation.* SARAH HARDING *clops in, her shawl around her.*

SARAH. Three small russets.

ANNIE. Where you been?

SARAH. That's all we needed . . .

ANNIE. Where? Where? (*She takes a swipe at* REGGIE *but he dodges.*) Stand still while I hit you!

RALPH. Play fair. Let him use his feet.

ANNIE. Shut up! You are going to stand still while I hit you. Will you stand still while I hit you? (*She takes a few more unsuccessful swipes.*)

Enter BERTHA TREECOTT.

BERTHA. Morning May. Can I have an orange? (*Seeing the fray:*) Oh lor!

ANNIE. He's defying me! Stand still! This is your mother telling you.

TOM. Russets, Sarah.

ANNIE. Will you stand still while I hit you!

SARAH. Putting us off our breakfasts!

ANNIE. Stays out with drunks. Yesterday he was tying
  doorknockers together. Pulled Mrs Hamilton's knocker right
  off.

RALPH. Did he be God? And her a devout Wesleyan!

ANNIE. Take your low morals to your own end. (*To* REGGIE:)
  Come here! (*Spotting her chance she dives in and clouts*
  REGGIE *repeatedly on the head*.) There! There! And
  that . . . and that. And take that dirty grin off your face. Oh
  you bugger!

  REGGIE *makes a fast exit.*

  Now he's made me swear! You witness he made me swear!

RALPH. Takes a lot to do that, Mrs Boggis.

  Factory hooters go off near and far.

MAY. Thank heavens!

BERTHA. Tom. My orange!

EVA. Did she have to hit that boy like that?

RALPH. Regular show that is. You'll see worse than that. Stand
  back for the rush. This is your clog chorus.

SARAH (*to* TOM): And one for me.

ANNIE. Plums!

MAY. No plums.

  A blackout as hooters and the roar of clogs reach a crescendo.

  Lights up on the stall ten minutes later.
  MAY *and* EVA *alone clearing the baskets away back on to
  the hand cart.*

MAY. No. All I have against the Accrington Pals is that they've
  taken the best men.

EVA. They volunteered.

MAY. Why? Educated boys like Tom and Ralph. You don't need qualifications to be shot at! Let those out of work go. The work-shy. Those who won't do a hand's turn. God knows there's enough of them.

EVA. Ralph was that fed up with the office.

MAY. Is that why? Oh these men . . . never happier than when they're arms round one another's necks, bawling good fellowship, in full retreat from what life's all about. Well Eva, what d'you think? (*She indicates the stall.*)

EVA. I should like to.

MAY. Should you? I've scarcely made ninepence this morning. It's hardly worth it . . . but you have to be here. And the girls like to pick up a bit extra to eat when they're out of the house, for they get little enough at home. All the tit-bits go to their fathers and the brothers get what's left. So maimed or halt you have to turn out in rain, frost or pitch black. I used to think it was mad getting up to sell apples and oranges by moonlight.

EVA. At least you've people to talk to. Putting cows in the shippin or out weeding kale on your own you go queer in the head. You get sick of being with yourself. And now Ralph won't be coming up on his bike I'm desperate to get away.

MAY. You're . . . not in any trouble?

EVA. Me? (*Realises.*) Oh no. We were always most careful . . .

MAY gives her a look.

I mean to avoid that kind of thing.

She is not very convincing.

MAY. Dear me. I've made myself blush.

EVA. I'm just glad to be in town.

MAY. Well you can still see the fields from most of the streets, even if you can't see them from here. Accrington's a site better than where Tom comes from. Oh the Hackfords! They had such a dreadful outlook. And such habits. They

can be very vile in Salford. No, these are not like the slums
he knew. Not slums at all. Not this end of the street at any
rate.

EVA. I always wanted to be where there was a bit of life.

MAY. Oh there's life here. Only walk up there a few yards and
it's falling out of the doorways on you. There's nothing
much you can do here but you're in the midst of life. You'd
better know what you're coming into. It's no Garden of
Eden. People are not paupers exactly, though some of them
behave as if they are. Those with the newspaper up at the
front windows. You can't be so poor that you can't find a
bit of net somewhere. The smell from them nauseates and
their children forever runny-nosed with lice and ringworm
and God knows. Oh and at the backs down the entries where
Ralph lives . . . have you seen? There's a lake of water,
if it is water, as black as treacle and what's in it I don't
know . . . such dead things and live things. It wants a river
of carbolic to wash it all away. So that's what you're
coming into and you must decide. And it's only part time as
you know.

EVA. You make it sound very bad.

MAY. I wish it were better.

EVA. And I know I'm a poor substitute for Tom.

MAY. What makes you say that?

EVA. Only that you must be sorry to see him go. Ralph told me
how you went to the recruiting office and tried to get him
off.

MAY. Did he? Tom's chosen to go. (*Smiles.*) Go round the back
to first gate. Door's open. Put the kettle on. Wiggle the raker
a bit but not too much or it'll burn away. We'll be comfortable
for an hour. (*Indicates hand cart.*) Put that in the yard where
you can see it or it will grow legs and walk.

EVA *pulls the cart off.*
MAY *laces up the covers of the stall. Presently she turns
thinking about her attempt to get* TOM *released. We now go
back in time to play that scene.*

As lights fade on the stall C.S.M. RIVERS *enters in his shirt sleeves, his collar turned down. He lathers his chin for shaving.*

Scene Two

MAY *moves slowly into the recruiting office.*

RIVERS. Yes M'am?

MAY. I should like to see the officer.

RIVERS. No officers present m'am. Will the warrant officer do?

MAY. If you please.

RIVERS. That is myself m'am. Company Sergeant Major Rivers. Would you take a seat while I finish the remaining whiskers? Leaving them only stiffens their resistance.

MAY *is suddenly shy of him. She sits. Then she gradually gets impatient.*

MAY. It's about a young boy you've recruited today.

RIVERS. Name?

MAY. I'd rather not give it at the moment.

RIVERS. Would that be because he gave a false statement concerning his age?

MAY. No! He's very truthful. He's nineteen.

RIVERS. Some would call him a man at that age, not a boy.

MAY. He's still an articled apprentice.

RIVERS *wipes his face and puts on his tunic.*

RIVERS. You are related to him.

MAY. Not . . . yes. I'm his cousin. Second cousin. But his parents are dead.

RIVERS. And you feel responsible for him. Well, that's a cold way of putting it. I'm sure that this young man is held very close in your affection.

MAY. He is an apprentice lithographic artist at Warrilows and he's thrown his future away!

RIVERS. And you keep a green grocery stall on the corner of Waterloo Street.

MAY. How did you know?

RIVERS. There's not much I've missed in this town m'am since I came. I was very impressed with your air of competence in running it.

MAY. He helped me with it.

RIVERS. And that helped him . . . not earning much from his apprenticeship.

MAY. He's too easily swayed. He's let others talk him into this.

RIVERS. These are upsetting times for us all. I can see you're surprised, me saying that when my job here is to imbue men with the spirit of duty and service. All the same I can sympathise. I was just on the point of retirement myself. Had in mind a little business . . . not unlike your own . . .

MAY. I'm explaining his situation.

RIVERS. He signed. Took the oath.

MAY.Egged on by others!

RIVERS. Oh m'am. If you knew some of the men I've had to make soldiers of in the past. Dregs and peelings of humanity, some of them, though they stood up well enough in the end. But here . . . they're paragons! Your Mayor calls for seven hundred volunteers from Accrington, Blackburn, Burnley, Chorley and hereabouts. They came in a matter of days . . . and all in such a spirit of cheerfulness and good humour. The smallest town in these islands to raise its own battalion. It make me humble.

MAY. He was drunk. He can't take drink!

RIVERS. No m'am. We wouldn't have allowed it. I see the homes these men come from where they have loved ones and are desperately needed. None were taken in drink.

MAY. I could pay the money back . . . what he was given . . .

RIVERS. There's no machinery for that. None at all.

MAY. I could pay you! I've money I was saving towards a shop.

RIVERS. Then I advise you to put it to that use. There's great satisfaction in keeping a shop. You have no one else dependent on you but him?

MAY shakes her head.

Then I will tell you what I'll do. I will make that young man my special charge. Hand your responsibility over to me and I shall not be found wanting. I shall be with him in every present danger . . . the darkest moments, you can be assured. Everything I've learned that has preserved me till now shall be at the disposal of one you feel so much towards . . .

MAY. I didn't say . . .

RIVERS. I shall be his very shadow.

MAY. But he's an artist. He's forgetful . . . he's no soldier!

RIVERS. That is my task.

MAY. He mustn't go!

RIVERS. He must. And into my care.

MAY. I want to see the officers.

RIVERS. By all means. They'll talk to you. They'll talk to you as though it was all a game . . . a sunlit meadow for bright-eyed lads to go running after honour and glory like happy footballers. But I don't talk like that to you because I believe that you and I have an understanding. I have more respect than to talk like that. Whatever I do is done with seriousness. I may say, with love. Leave him to me.

MAY is spent and confused by his manner. Something about him makes her unsure of herself.

MAY. But you don't know his name.

RIVERS. I think I do. I think I do, madam.

MAY. Tom Hackford.

RIVERS. Private Hackford. Yes m'am.

As MAY goes . . . Blackout.

Scene Three

The stall. Mid-morning. EVA, SARAH *and* BERTHA.

SARAH. Where's that man? I get home specially to see him off and where is he?

BERTHA. You just don't know them anymore! They even walk different.

SARAH. Well they think they're it, don't they?

BERTHA. My own father come round the corner and I didn't know him at first. They look so swaggery in them uniforms. And Ralph!

SARAH. Him! I've never known a man with such a talent for turning up everywhere at once. And he's that full of farewells.

EVA. You mean kissing all the lips on offer.

SARAH. D'you mind?

EVA. No. Minding won't change him will it?

SARAH. But he's very good. He's said 'goodbye' twice to my mother and he can't stand the sight of her. Has Madam left you in charge then?

EVA. No. It's not settled yet. She's just getting some plums.

BERTHA. I feel neither use nor ornament. They go off and do it all and I stay here and do nothing.

SARAH. You do a full shift on the looms while they'll be playing around in tents.

BERTHA. They're going to fight the Germans.

SARAH. In Caernarvon? The only fighting they'll do is with

those Welsh women. The advance party said some of them
are that wild they can't speak two words of English. One
sight of soldiers and they pour down from the hills in droves.

BERTHA. Droves! Are they like that?

SARAH. I can't see my Bill putting up much resistance. Still,
it'll be over before he gets his oats.

BERTHA. Sarah!

EVA. D'you think so?

SARAH. I've heard that our Royal family is having talks with
the German Royal family. They're related. Isn't as if we're
fighting France where they've got no royalty at all! The
main thing I've got against the Kaiser is that he didn't declare
war three year ago. Because then I wouldn't have got a kid
and got married.

EVA (to BERTHA): What would you do if you could?

BERTHA. I'd be a nurse.

SARAH. What d'you know to be a nurse? It's all ladies going to
be nurses. Ladies and horribles. Sick of seeing their photos
in the paper. The horrible Miss Snitch seen here tending
lightly wounded at Lady Snot's country seat.

BERTHA. If I could, I would. Oh those awful, hateful Germans!

RALPH enters and sweeps EVA up into an embrace.

RALPH. It's Accrington Carnival and Fête. You can't get down
the street.

BERTHA. Did you hear Ralph?

RALPH. Poor old Arthur's in a state bidding adieu to his
pigeons. Did I hear what, love?

BERTHA. The Germans. There was a picture in the local
from the War Illustrated. There were these British Tommies
digging trenches in Belgium. Along comes a funeral
procession from the village down the road . . . all Belgium
people dressed in black. All our men take off their caps and
stand in respect. Suddenly off comes the lid of the coffin
and there's two great Germans with a machine gun. Shot

them all down!

RALPH. Don't worry Bertha. We shall send them home in coffins they can't get out of. Where's Tom? Tom! I asked him to do a quick sketch of you so I could take it with me.

EVA. Yes he did start it but I told him not to bother. He wanted to pack.

RALPH. What? (*Calls again.*) Tom! Out here with you!

SARAH (*uncertain*): How d'you get two Germans and a machine gun in a coffin?

Drums start up in a neighbouring street.

RALPH. There's the Boy's Brigade. When we heard there wasn't going to be a band at the station to see us off, Harry Leatherbarrel says: 'the hell we'll have no band. Get the brigade out!'

Bugles play a march. The girls climb on the stall to get a view.

SARAH. Blow, boys . . . blow!

BERTHA. Oooh! Frank's on the big drum!

TOM has entered in full kit.

RALPH. That sketch Thomas!

TOM gets out a pad and pencil.

EVA. Don't be so overbearing!

TOM. Sitting by the stall just as you were before.

The girls sing with the bugles:

SARAH. ⎫ I've joined the Boy's Brigade,
BERTHA. ⎭ They call me marmalade.
        I hit me bum instead of me drum
        I've joined the Boy's Brigade.

TOM. Could you lay your left hand on the counter? More this way.

RALPH. My little pocket Venus! My rose of Clayton-le-Moors!

SARAH. Me next Tom.

RALPH. He's only time for one . . . as I have.

SARAH. Oh yes?

Enter REGGIE *in Boy's Brigade regalia pursued by* ANNIE. ARTHUR *brings up the rear in full kit plus a pigeon in a basket.*

ANNIE. Run you daft thing. They'll be miles off! Slowcoach! Couldn't find his mouthpiece.

RALPH. Can you blow it Reggie?

REGGIE *does a quick blast on the bugle.*

REGGIE. You just press your lips, tight, like, and do a sort of farting sound.

ANNIE. Get off! (*She takes a swipe at him as he goes.*)

(*To* ARTHUR:) And you stand by and let him defy me! What are you going to do to those Huns if you can't lift a finger to your own child?

ARTHUR. Christ said . . .

ANNIE. Christ said suffer the children. *Suffer* them!

RALPH. You're in Tom's way. The artist is at work.

ANNIE (*delivering the word like an insult*): Artist!

SARAH. Is it true that when you were at Accrington Art School they let you draw girls undressed?

She is doing this to anger ANNIE. MAY *enters and stays to one side watching.*

TOM. No. It isn't. They were draped.

ANNIE. 'Draped' . . . well we all know what that means don't we?

BERTHA (*genuinely interested*): No.

RALPH. It means covered up so you can still see everything. Tom has the artist's eye. He can look at any woman . . . any woman . . . and see her in the softly shaded form that nature first bestowed.

ANNIE. If you worked like a woman works you'd have nothing

left 'bestowed' at all.

ARTHUR (*peering at the sketch*): You have a gift Tom. A divine gift.

   EVA *comes over to see. The others gather round.*

EVA. I've never been sketched ever. What's it like?

BERTHA. Isn't it wonderful!

TOM. The hands aren't right. There's a knack of getting hands . . .

SARAH. But the face!

BERTHA (*to* MAY): Say he's clever.

MAY. I never denied it.

TOM. I'll finish off the shading when we're at camp.

EVA. I don't know what to say.

RALPH. Put your lips to it.

EVA. What?

RALPH. Put your lips to it and I'll treasure it.

BERTHA. Oh go on!

EVA. Will it smudge?

TOM. No.

   EVA *gently kisses the sketch. The others respond.*

BERTHA. Oh how romantic!

SARAH My knees have turned to water.

   We hear the Boy's Brigade wheeling round the streets audible again.

RALPH. They're coming back round.

SARAH. I must see Bill . . . Goodbye Ralph. Be good Tom (*She kisses them.*) Arthur, I'll kiss your cheek. Goodbye!

   She goes.

ARTHUR. God go with you Sarah.

BERTHA. Are you taking that pigeon Mr Boggis?

ARTHUR. Oh, I couldn't leave this one.

ANNIE. The others have gone to his brother Bert. I'd have plucked and stuffed them and put them in pies else.

ARTHUR. England's Glory. I call her that because she's a match for any bird. Now before we go I should like us all to stand for a moment in prayer.

ANNIE. Not in the street.

ARTHUR. It's God's street.

RALPH. Go on. I've shut my eyes.

ARTHUR. Well God. Here we are in your town, in your kingdom, in the midst of your creation, which, despite these shadows come upon us, despite the prison walls of life that surround us, looks lovely yet. You smile, I know. For we are men without craft or guile called to do your work in far off places. Bless the women who stay, your handmaidens, for it is they who tend our homes and loved ones now. Keep us in their thoughts as they in ours and our feet to the paths of righteousness, amen.

ALL. Amen.

Each has reacted in his or her own way, TOM *most embarrassed, torn between his unbelief and his natural politeness.*

RALPH. You should preach at the Ebenezer.

ANNIE. And would have if he wasn't such a muggins as to be a Primitive.

RALPH. Let's get the train. Shut the stall.

MAY. No. Leave it.

RALPH. You're coming aren't you?

MAY. You go Eva. I'll see to things here.

RALPH. But you've got to come.

MAY. Got to?

RALPH. Can't you ever stop — One hour! Tom!

TOM. Not if she doesn't want to.

An uncomfortable moment.

BERTHA. My father'll wonder where on earth I am.

ANNIE. Arthur!

ARTHUR. Goodbye May. His ways are mysterious. He makes a worker of you and a soldier of me. His will be done.

MAY. Come home safely Arthur.

BERTHA (*to* TOM *and* RALPH): I'll see you at the station.

ARTHUR *sets off in soldierly fashion,* ANNIE *following with* BERTHA.

ANNIE. Don't march! I'm not marching!

EVA *has been signalling* RALPH *to make amends.*

RALPH (*to* MAY): Sorry I spoke. If you don't want to . . . it's your pleasings.

MAY. Nothing stops. Nothing! Not for the Pals. Not for the war. Not if every man in the town went to it. You can throw whatever you like away for seven shillings a week. Not here. They'll feed you and shelter you. Not here. That has to be got every minute of the day. No one gets it for you.

RALPH. You're still the Tartar of Waterloo Street. Good luck to you May.

RALPH *and* EVA *go.*

TOM. Shall I chuck it?

MAY. What?

TOM. Shall I not go?

MAY. And go to clink?

TOM. I could run my head against that wall!

MAY. This is the mood you've put me in. It's no use me standing on that platform waving a hanky and singing Auld Lang Syne or God Save the King. I don't feel especially proud of myself and I wish I could do otherwise.

TOM. Shall I be able to drop in . . . on leave?

MAY. Providing Eva's with me and you're prepared to sleep on the sofa. But not if the house is empty. Not again.

TOM. I must thank you for taking me in and all that.

MAY *takes an envelope out of her pocket and thrusts it at him.*

MAY. Put this in your pocket.

TOM. What is it?

MAY. Put it away.

TOM. Not if it's money.

MAY. It's four pounds that's all.

TOM. Take it back.

MAY. I wanted to give you something.

TOM *stares at her. The bugle band gets louder as it passes the end of the street.* TOM *suddenly tries to embrace her but* MAY *isn't able to respond. She pushes him away.* TOM *can't give in and struggles with her but* MAY *is frantic and strong. As the bugles blare they keep up this silent wrestling with one another. Finally* TOM *breaks away.*

TOM. Yes, you'll give me money! You'll give me money all right!

He goes to the stall, takes an apple, bites it. Then he takes the envelope she gave him and slams it down on the stall. Then goes.

MAY *is left trembling with fear at what they have done.*

Blackout.

Scene Four

MAY's *kitchen, three months later.*
      EVA *and* SARAH *enter having just got home from the mill.*
      EVA *lights a lamp.*

SARAH. I'm dying for a bit of warmth!

EVA. It cuts you right in two.

SARAH. Quick then before May comes back and finds me in her kitchen.

      EVA *gets a copy of The Accrington Observer.*

      Lord how I've hated this winter. I's'll have to hem up this skirt again. I'm sick of slush and frozen feet. And me empty bed all these months. Just me and a bloody hot brick . . . I'll go potty. I'll have to do something. I'd join some fat Sultan's harem to get warmed up again, I would. Silk sheets, boxes of dates and an emerald in your navel!! Have you found it?

EVA. There's a bit about the Pals at camp.

SARAH. There always is. Read me the funny poem.

EVA. You might not think it funny . . .

SARAH. Read it.

EVA (*reads*):
      Oh where are those Russians,
      Those hairy faced Russians,
      Who sailed from Archangel and landed in Leith?
      Who came over in millions,
      Some say, sir, in trillions,
      With big furry caps and armed to the teeth.
      Pray where have you put them,
      Or shipped them or shut them
      In England, France, Belgium, or in Timbuctoo?
      For 'tis tantalising
      Thus daily surmising,
      Come dear Mr Censor pray tell us now do!

SARAH. Oh that's good! Who's it by?

EVA. T. Clayton.

SARAH. He's clever. And you know I've met plenty who
believed it. There was a train driver who swore he'd seen
them. A thousand Cossacks on Manchester Central
Station . . . and with snow on their boots. As though they'd
send them over here.

EVA. But if you're never told anything. Mary Cotteril's brother
was stopped putting word in his letters home about the rats
and lice in the trenches. The officer said he had to put
uplifting things about how cheerful they all are.

SARAH. Well I'd better relieve me mother of the kids though
I'm certain I'm too tired to face them.

EVA. Stay a bit. Kettle's on.

SARAH. It's May's evening for seeing her paying customers
isn't it?

EVA. Who?

SARAH. Don't pretend. The posh lot up Peel Park way. We
know. If anything's in short supply . . . sugar or caulies . . .
she buys off she knows at the market and sneaks it
off to her special ladies for a good profit.

EVA. She wants me to go up there.

SARAH. Don't. They should put that lot to work. With their
Tipparary Clubs and their comforts for the troops. They've
started a sewing and knitting circle for making sandbags and
socks and the way they do them you can't tell one from
t'other.

EVA *laughs, then shudders.*

EVA. Thank God the Pals are still in England.

SARAH. Miss him?

EVA *nods.*

I saw a sailor, home on leave from the Warspite. He was
walking with that wiggle . . . you know how they do? I went
ting-a-ling all the way to the bread shop.

EVA *suddenly hears something.*

EVA. May!

SARAH. Read something . . . anything.

MAY *enters as* EVA *reads.*

EVA. 'Pals Inspected By The Duke of Connaught. The 11th East Lancs, our own Accrington Pals made a splendidly disciplined sight . . .' Oh May . . . I was just going to make the tea.

MAY. I'll do that. Hello Sarah.

SARAH. I only slipped in on the way back from the mill to hear the bits of news.

MAY. You're very welcome.

SARAH *exchanges a look of surprise with* EVA.

Did you read her the poem, Eva?

EVA. Yes.

MAY. Oh isn't he good that man? And she's such a good reader. I saw crocuses in the park. That's a hopeful sign, isn't it?

SARAH. Well I was just saying how we needed an end to the cold . . . and so on.

MAY. I had a word from Tom today.

EVA. Did you?

MAY. Well he doesn't write much.

SARAH. Oh they're shocking that way.

MAY. She gets reams from Ralph. No, Tom just says how he likes the Welsh people and how they all stood in a crowd outside Caernarvon Castle and sang hymns . . . and he joined in. Tom singing hymns! He said he'd never heard such singing and, you know, he's got a very fine baritone voice. Oh Eva, if he were here you could do duets, for she sings beautifully. I shall have to practise the piano so I can play for you.

During this MAY *makes the tea.*

SARAH. Wouldn't that be nice?

MAY. Will you have a cup?

SARAH (*surprised*): Oh! Well . . . no, thank you very much. My mother . . . and I've such work to do. Endless mending. There's nothing left in the seat of Albert's trousers but mending. You end up mending the mending and darning the darns. So . . . I'd better be off.

MAY. But do drop in any time, won't you?

As she goes SARAH *gives* EVA *a puzzled look.*

SARAH. I will. Ta-ta!

She goes. MAY *resumes her more accustomed style.*

MAY. It'll be a relief to her not to have to poke her nose in from outside the window. She can come and do it indoors.

EVA. Now you've spoiled it!

MAY. I have, haven't I? Keep trying to reform me. You never know.

EVA. Will you have a bun? I got some.

MAY. You see! Rolling in it now. How was work?

EVA. Awful. Foreman teases me.

MAY. Jack Proudlove?

EVA. Calls me the milkmaid.

MAY. Tease him about dyeing his hair.

EVA. He dyes his hair?

MAY. Didn't you know? Uses soot and butter.

EVA. Is he that vain?

MAY. Oh no. It's not vanity. It's so the bosses won't notice his age. Quite a few of the older ones do it. It's a hard life.

EVA. It is.

MAY. While I was out I looked at a shop or two . . . the ones I've fancied taking on, you know. And suddenly it all seems more possible. I never believed the war would make a difference like this. There's money around. The mills are back . . . engineering, munitions. And there's shops that fell empty in the hard times you could have for really low rents.

EVA. But you don't want it to go on?

MAY. Not to take Tom and Ralph, no. Just long enough so's I
can afford the stock. We'll be singing round the piano yet.
Round here they think I'm queer in the head having a piano.
But I could never let it go. It was my father's. When I was
small we were quite up in the world. Lower-middle class.
My father used to say upper-working but mother said lower-
middle. We lived in one of those villas in Hendal Street . . .
before it went downhill. But then father got this notion of
speculating in second-hand pianos and that was his undoing.
Lost money on them. Lost his job at Paxton's through
slipping out to do deals. Did all kinds of jobs after that. Oh
he was a character! He once worked for a photographer's
shop. Now lots of people who had photos taken never
paid up. So, one week while father was in charge of the
shop he put all these people's photos in the window with
the backs turned to the street so you couldn't see the faces
and a notice saying if they didn't pay up by Saturday the
photos would be turned round. Sparks flew then! He got the
sack. But then my mother, who was a very simple soul, and
danced attendance on him, morning, noon and night . . .
well when she died it seemed she'd secretly managed to
scrimp and save a bit of money and it looked like father and
me might get a shop . . . a piano shop. But he frittered most
of it away. Then he rented the stall like I told you. Took me
from the mill to help run it. He just wouldn't do that kind of
work. Went into a depression. I ended up keeping him till
he died. You won't pass any of this on will you?

EVA. Of course not.

MAY. I trust you, you know. He used to love Shakespeare.
Took Tom and me once or twice when the players came. But
he'd get drunk and whenever the actors got their lines wrong
he'd stand up and correct them.

EVA. They wouldn't like that!

MAY. They didn't! He'd be thrown out and we'd hide under
the seats pretending we weren't with him, hoping to see the

rest. Oh . . . Ophelia . . . Ophelia. And Tom's a dreamer just like father was. That's what worries me.

EVA. D'you think Ralph might forget me? We've scarcely been going together three months.

MAY. If he forgets you then you forget him!

EVA. Can't.

She holds up her hands spaced apart.

D'you see that? That's the distance from his right shoulder to his left. Am I silly?

MAY. Yes. If you want an honest answer.

EVA. Look . . .

She makes shapes with her hands.

There's his arms. There's his chest.

MAY. I don't want to talk about them all the time. I have my cash book to do.

EVA. I've made up my mind to be truthful. I could have given the wrong impression. I have slept with him.

MAY. You don't mean it?

EVA. I wouldn't want others to tell you. So if you want me to go.

MAY. You've given yourself?

EVA *can't hide a smile.*

Have I said something funny?

EVA. No. I just hadn't thought of it as 'giving'. If you'd seen him as I have,

MAY. Well, as you say he's got arms and a chest. They all have, haven't they? But I'm a bit shocked that you should think I'd want you to go whatever you've done. I'm not very experienced in that way. What I know about men you could put into a thimble. Still, I hope I'm not a prude. Yet there are facts. At Paxtons . . . they don't pay you what they'd pay a man, do they?

EVA. No they don't!

MAY. And never will. You'll always have the rags and tags.
So, unless you've some form of independence you have to
be dependent on some man or other. And if you lose . . .
that . . . they won't look at you. But don't listen to me. There
was only the once with them . . . and that I don't brag about.

She notes EVA's *look.*

Oh not Tom! Before I knew him. You didn't think that?
Tom! I could never spoil his life!

EVA. How d'you mean 'spoil'?

MAY. I'm ten years older! And how could I live with such a
soft thing? When he first came and was at Accrington Station,
just off the train, a Salvation Army man came up to him
and said: 'Have you found the Lord?' And Tom says: 'No,
I've only just arrived'.

EVA. What a shame!

MAY. Well, let's leave the subject. Tell me, while I think about it,
d'you know what Esperanto is?

EVA. Esperanto?

MAY. Is it that language?

EVA. I think so . . .

MAY. I must find out. Mrs Dickenson, Alderman Dickenson's
wife, had a chat while I was on my rounds. Amongst other
things she mentioned that she was secretary of the local
Esperanto Society. I didn't know what to say. I did feel a
fool. Whatever it was it took her to Paris just before the war.
I told her about you.

EVA. Me?

MAY. Your singing. They run concerts for raising funds. For
the troops.

EVA. Oh you never said I'd sing?

MAY. I didn't push it. But you could get asked. It's the way to
get on. When I think how my father and me came to this

door with our furniture and I saw how mean and small it was with its broken quarries and dark little stairs and I said never, never, never will I stay. (*Pause.*) You get yourself ready for bed. I'll do my cash.

EVA. I'm relieved I told you about Ralph.

MAY. Are you?

EVA. I don't like secrets.

> EVA *hovers.* MAY *gets her cash book and settles down at the table.*

D'you think they are moving them from Caernarvon to Staffordshire?

MAY. It's what it says in the paper.

EVA. But supposing that they're just covering up that they're moving them to France.

MAY. They wouldn't do that. If they were moving them to France they'd say nothing. They wouldn't make up a story. Don't start decrying authority like Sarah does. That's silly. You can bake your cake. He'll be here on leave.

EVA. And Tom.

MAY. No. He'll go to Salford.

> EVA *goes.* MAY *remains finishing her books. She lowers the lamp.*

> *By the tarpaulin on the fruit stall* TOM *is revealed in greatcoat and full equipment. He is on guard duty at the training camp. Silence as he stares ahead and* MAY *makes entries in her book. Then she closes the book, stands and, taking her lamp, goes.*

Scene Five

SERGEANT-MAJOR RIVERS *moves to* TOM's *side. He speaks very softly.*

RIVERS: Guard . . .

TOM. Sir!

RIVERS. Keep it quiet. Guard . . . attention! Stand at ease. Easy. Are you, guard, fully instructed in the procedure of challenge and recognition?

TOM. Yes sir.

RIVERS. Make your report.

TOM. Nothing sir. Just two men on bikes, sir, ten minutes ago.

RIVERS. What kind of men?

TOM. From the village sir . . .

RIVERS. What kind of men?

TOM. Farm workers, sir. From the Green Dragon, sir.

RIVERS. Without looking at your rifle tell me . . . is the safety catch applied?

TOM. Yes . . . sir.

RIVERS. Now look.

TOM *looks at his rifle and realises the catch is 'on'.*

Apply it. That's a chargeable offence, Private Hackford.

TOM. Yes sir. (*He applies the catch.*)

RIVERS. We don't want you shooting yourself in the head. Shoot the enemy not yourself. You're on our side. It must always be second nature to know the state of preparedness of your rifle. Make it an instinct. We don't usually have the luxury of thought when the time comes. You've good visibility . . . clear moon.

TOM. Yes sir.

RIVERS. Clear, but small. Remote. I've seen moons over the Sudanese desert you could reach out and touch. Have you heard from Miss Hassal?

TOM. Just a few lines sir.

RIVERS. I trust she's in health?

TOM. Oh yes sir.

RIVERS. Now guard. What can you hear?

TOM. Nothing sir . . .

RIVERS. You can hear men sleeping. Seven hundred men
kipping like babies . . . deep in the land of nod . . . all tucked
up in their pits . . . and each and every one of those men is
depending on your eyes and ears. That's what soldiering's
about . . . comradeship. So that some night when you've got
your head down you know that there's a man out there
who'll look out for you, no matter what. That's where we're
different from civvy street. No one can divide us from each
other. What dismays an enemy is the knowledge that every
man he faces on the other side is loyal and attentive to his
fellow at all times . . . not because he's ordered to be so . . .
but out of the love he bears his brother in arms. Guard!
Guard attention! Guard . . . stand at ease! Guard carry on.

As RIVERS *goes and* TOM *stands guard a light begins to
grow around the table in* MAY's *kitchen. Gradually* TOM
becomes aware of it.

Scene Six

TOM *moves slowly towards the table. He looses off his
equipment and places it on a chair with his rifle. He hangs up
his greatcoat and, removing his tunic, places it over the back of
a chair. All the time he is listening as a man does in a sleeping
house. He sits at the table. From above we hear* EVA *and*
RALPH . . . *muffled laughter followed by* EVA *shushing*
RALPH . . . *then* RALPH *murmuring:* My love. Oh my love!
MAY *enters with a lamp. She is in her nightdress with a coat
over it.*

MAY. Can't you sleep?

TOM. I just thought I'd sit in the kitchen . . .

She looks up at the ceiling, nervously, then sits at the table. Another burst of laughter from upstairs.

MAY. Whatever shall I do? I shouldn't have let them, should I? I said to him: Ralph it's eleven o'clock. He says: Right, I'm going and then trots off up the stairs! Oooh, he's got some face! I haven't shut my eyes. But it's funny too . . .

TOM. What makes you laugh?

MAY. That leg of the bed you mended. It's never been right. I kept thinking: It'll come off! It'll have them over! (*Pause.*) All these months she's been like a sister to me. I can refuse her nothing . . . nothing at all. Yet it is wrong of them. I always thought there was more to her than there seemed to be when she first came. She's so 'open' . . . no, I don't mean 'open' . . . so 'level'. She'll sit where you are of an evening and I'll find myself doing all the talking. And she'll smile and she'll listen and she'll comment . . . sensibly . . . and all the time she's being exactly herself . . . never putting on, or saying things for effect. (*Listens.*) Here . . . are they asleep?

TOM. Aye. I think so. In the arms of Morpheus.

MAY. Morpheus? Is that what it is? Well I hope they are for old Mrs Big Ears next door can put a cup to the wall and catch everything.

She gets up, uncertainly, then goes into the scullery and returns with some flowers and wire.

Shouldn't you try and get some sleep?

TOM. In a bit. What are those?

MAY. Nosegays. I've had an order for a wedding. Buttonholes and corsage. It's years since I did any.

TOM. Whose wedding?

MAY. Oh, not round here. Mrs Dickenson's niece is marrying an officer from the King's Own Liverpools.

TOM. I must pay you something, May.

MAY. What for?

TOM. Staying here.

MAY. Don't insult me. Your money should go to Salford to your aunt . . . who must wonder why you spend your leave here and not there.

TOM. She gets my allowance. Hardly spend a bean at camp. You don't need to. That's the great thing about the army. You don't need money. Everything's found. It's an exchange. It's really opened my eyes. I mean it proves it . . .

MAY. Proves what?

TOM. That money's not needed. It's not necessary. Not really. People think it is because they're too boneheaded to see . . . that it isn't. It gets in the way!

MAY. Don't raise your voice!

TOM. It's a free exchange of skills . . . of produce of hand or brain. That's what's needed. Not money. (*Indicates flowers*.) The skill you put into that . . . to exchange it freely for that which you need in return.

MAY. And what do I need?

TOM *is stopped by this.*

Dreamer.

He reaches for a nosegay. MAY is on edge and starts as he comes close.

TOM. I should have picked you some in Staffordshire.

MAY. I always think of it as Black Country.

TOM. No . . . not Penkridge. It's a picture. There's a lake. I've tried to do it water colour, but there's a real knack in getting reflections. I should get oils.

MAY. How much do oils cost?

TOM *suddenly takes her hand awkwardly.*

No . . . no . . .

TOM. They're up there.

MAY. I know they're up there. Girls used to be taught to show restraint. To be 'spiritual'. Now they say 'What use is it thinking like that anymore?

TOM. Then what use is it?

MAY. I must go upstairs and you should try to get some sleep in the parlour.

She goes to the bedroom door. She pauses.

Tom . . . would you do a sketch of me?

TOM. Now?

MAY. No, not now. While you're here. You've sketched Eva . . . but you've never done a likeness of me, have you?

TOM (*bitterly*): How d'you want it?

MAY. What d'you mean?

TOM. 'Spiritual'?

MAY. I said it was how we were taught.

TOM. As the Lady of the Lake . . . or the Angel of Mons?

MAY. Oh Tom! Do you think me so silly?

MAY *comes to him. He clings to her.*

TOM. I can't draw spirit . . . I can only draw your face . . . and your body . . .

MAY. If I'd only known you now! If I'd only known you as you are now. Why did you have to come here as a boy?

She takes his arms from her and goes off.
TOM *remains as lights fade.*

Scene Seven

ARTHUR *is revealed to one side of the stage. He is in uniform. His pigeon basket containing England's Glory is at his side. He speaks a letter he has written home.*

ARTHUR. To Jack Burndred, 14 Waterloo Street, Accrington, Lancs. Dear brother in Christ, as you will have read in the local the Pals have moved on from Penkridge to the cathedral city of Ripon. I regret the change. It is a move from God's cathedral of green fields and trees to the cathedral of the bishops. However, Ripon is a splendid garden city and lit by the new wonder of electric street lighting. Surely when we make progress like this shall we not ask: where is the progress we should be making towards the new Jerusalem?

The Pals were inspected by Lieutenant Colonel Sir Archibald J. Murrary KCB DSO who said it was the finest Kitchener battalion he had ever seen . . . and he has inspected not thousands . . . but tens of thousands.

Thank you for asking after England's Glory who is in fine fettle and makes our feathered friends in the battalion signals loft look a moth-eaten set by comparison. Thank you also for the news from the works. I was indignant to hear how the masters were still behaving, but God sees them, how they have sinned in the unacceptable manipulation of piece work rates in the finishing shop. There is not a quarter of a farthing wrongfully withheld from working men that He does not see.

You ask how I can bring myself to take up arms. I say how can I not when my fellows do? We have failed to build Jerusalem and this is God's answer. It is his second flood, though now by steel instead of water. Who has been perfect in God? Not me, for one. Sometimes I think the Vale of Sorrow I have known in the circumstances of my life tempted me away. Please ask Ethel to visit Annie and do what she can for the little ones and poor Reggie.

Well, God has called me to the lists and if I fall let my death help to cleanse the world of its weakness. I will close with the words of his purest handmaiden, Joanna Southcott:

'And now if foes increase, I'll tell you here,
That every sorrow they shall fast increase,
The wars their tumults they shall never cease
Until the hearts of men will turn to me.'
Yours in the sight of the Lord, Arthur Boggis.

Lights fade on ARTHUR *and fade up on the fruit stall for:*

Scene Eight

Winter 1915. EVA *is at the stall.* SARAH *brings on* BERTHA *who is wearing a tram conductress's uniform.*

SARAH. Have you seen this Eva? Have you seen what she's gone and done? (*To* BERTHA:) Stand up straight. You're not standing up straight.

EVA. It does look nice on you Bertha.

SARAH. Nice? Look at her.

BERTHA. She's aggravating me.

SARAH. Don't tell me you haven't noticed!

EVA. What?

SARAH. She's shortened the skirt!

BERTHA. Not much . . .

SARAH. Twelve inches off the ground! I thought I was going it with ten! You racy little thing . . . and stop bending at the knees. If you're going to be fast, be fast. Flash your boots for us. Come on!

BERTHA *does a quick kick.*

EVA. Oh and you took in the jacket then?

BERTHA. And got in trouble for it. But it was that baggy.

SARAH. I thought it was for selling tram tickets not driving the male population mad.

BERTHA. Me? Even my father says I'm better followed than faced.

SARAH. What does he know? Two pounds of King Edwards. I'll pick 'em myself.

EVA. Is it getting any better?

BERTHA. Not much. The men are such beasts about it.

SARAH. Who are?

BERTHA. Inspectors and drivers. Drivers are worst. Mine's forever slamming the brakes on to have me fall over. Won't speak to me hardly . . . and they won't have girls in the rest room except to get our tea. Then they dock our pay cos they say we have to have assistance with the poles, turning the trams round at the terminus.

SARAH. Oh they would have to cheat you. Would you credit the way they go on?

BERTHA. They say we're taking jobs off them and that we'll want to be drivers next.

SARAH. And why shouldn't you? If there's one thing that narks the men about this war it's the way it shows them up for creating such mysteries round things. My God! Providing both your eyes point forwards and your arms aren't stuck on back to front, anyone can drive a tram! Especially with their skirt twelve inches off the ground.

BERTHA. I don't want to drive a tram.

SARAH. You rabbit! Still neither would I. I'd be a female lumberjack if I could . . . in the Forestry . . . if I hadn't my own burdens.

EVA. I suppose they're afraid really.

SARAH. Who?

EVA. The men. Of being displaced. Now there's conscription coming, if women take their jobs they'll have to go.

SARAH. So they should!

BERTHA. They can take some that I know!

EVA. Yes but they have to face getting killed. We don't.

BERTHA. What a thing to say!

SARAH. What about the munitions girls . . . the girls in Gretna that got blown to bits that they tried to hush up? And getting canary through working with TNT so you're coughing yellow cud the rest of your life?

BERTHA. You make me feel I've done wrong.

EVA. I didn't mean to . . .

SARAH. Come on Bertha. (*To* EVA:) You! You get yourself stuck here when there's so much you could do.

EVA. I'm not 'stuck'.

SARAH. I bet her nibs doesn't think so. She's got you.

EVA. It's not like that Sarah. I'm perfectly free. And I'd feel perfectly content in a way. At least we're all together. If I think back to home now all I remember is the dark. Whatever you say, Sarah, we've got what matters most.

SARAH. Well I never knew I was well off!

Enter ANNIE BOGGIS.

ANNIE. Have you seen Reggie? Blast him, I'll break his flaming neck!

SARAH. Oh can't you stop harrying him for a moment?

ANNIE. Harrying?

SARAH. Every minute of the day!

ANNIE. Harrying?

SARAH. Forget I spoke.

ANNIE. I want to know what you mean by 'harrying'.

SARAH. Never mind.

ANNIE. Bertha! What does she mean?

BERTHA. Honestly Mrs Boggis, I don't know what it means either . . .

ANNIE. I know what *it* means you goof! I want to know what *she* means.

SARAH. For the Lord's sake.

Enter MAY *with the hand cart.*

ANNIE (*to* SARAH): Miss Piss! Well, your games are over. (*To* EVA:) And yours Mary from the Dairy. I see what goes on, broad as daylight. Still that's over now. Your games are over.

MAY. What games Annie?

ANNIE. I don't have to tell you. It's over. All over. It's come at last. They're to be shipped. Three weeks and the Pals'll be shipped off to France. Yes . . . I can see you didn't know.

SARAH. Who says?

ANNIE. Town Hall. Mrs Henshall got it from the bobby this afternoon. I left Reggie in the house and went up with her to see if it was right. Shipped to the bloody slaughter the lot of them.

MAY. It's true. They're going.

SARAH. There was nothing in the paper.

ANNIE. When is there ever? We got Mr Tenkerton out of the clerks office. They've got it in writing.

EVA. I shouldn't have said I was happy.

BERTHA. I must go . . . mother'll be out of her mind!

SARAH. The kids! Come on Bertha!

SARAH *and* BERTHA *go.*

ANNIE. Now you'll see some 'harrying'. Now you'll be learned what it means. Oh you'll be learned! (*Calls:*) Reggie!

MAY *inspects the cash box.*

MAY. You've not taken much.

EVA. Have they got leave?

MAY. Apparently. Some of them. Oh he'll come. But I wouldn't blame Tom if he didn't. I think you're wiser than I am. Least you're not going to look back and think Ralph volunteered because you were cold to him.

MAY *busies herself with packing up the stall.*
Blackout.

Scene Nine

MAY's *kitchen some weeks later.* RALPH *is washing himself with soap and flannel in a tin bath.* TOM *is repairing one of* MAY's *boots. He has a cobbler's last held between his knees and is nailing a new leather sole on to the uppers, a biscuit tin of tools and bits of leather to hand.*
RALPH *starts to make waves.*

RALPH. Swim for it! Swim for the shore! They see the rockets from the stricken ship. The wild North Easter blows it to the fang shaped rocks. They're lost! Then Grace Darling leaps to the oars of her frail craft. Pull! Pull! By God it's parky in here. Brrrr!

TOM. This is past mending with nails. It should be stitched if I had the thread.

He trims the edge of the sole with a sharp knife. RALPH *winces.*

RALPH. Here! Keep a good grip on that won't you? Bloody hell! Eva! Got any more hot?

EVA *pops her head in from the scullery.*

EVA. There's a jug of warm if you're ready for rinsing.

RALPH. Hot, I said.

EVA. You've had all there is that I'm letting you have. May'll go mad. Shall I come in?

TOM, *filling the leather sole, flinches uneasily.*

RALPH. I'm in my skin.

EVA. I know! (*Entering.*) You don't mind do you Tom?

TOM. Er . . . no. Carry on. I'll finish.

RALPH. Nothing deflects the craftsman from his task.

EVA. You do look a cherub!

RALPH. I feel a brass monkey. I'm starved.

EVA. No more hot. I'll soap your back. Lean over. Isn't he lovely? Don't you think Tom? Isn't he perfectly proportioned?

RALPH. Shut up! You'll worry him.

TOM. His arms are too short.

RALPH. What?

TOM. For perfect proportion.

RALPH. Too short?

TOM. If you look at Leonardo da Vinci's drawings . . . the tip of the middle finger reaches further down the thigh bone.

RALPH. Bugger Leonardo!

TOM goes out to the scullery for his cobbler's wax.

EVA. Let me feel that hollow in your back. Hmmm. That's mine that is.

She kisses him.

RALPH. The miner's dream of home!

She tips the jug of water over him.

Here . . . my arms aren't too short are they?

EVA. They can't be can they? They get everywhere.

The back gate slams. TOM reappears.

TOM. Hey-up. It's May.

EVA. Oh no!

RALPH. Towel!

EVA (*calling*): May! Don't come in. Ralph's in the bath.

MAY enters briskly with a shopping bag.

MAY. Ralph's what? Oh my Lord!

Unable to retreat, she turns her back.

RALPH. I'm sorry May, Our bath's got a leak in it.

EVA. And this one's got a parsnip.

MAY. Has he taken all the hot water?

EVA. I've rationed him.

RALPH. Isn't there a bigger flannel than this?

TOM. I'll hold the towel.

He holds it like a screen in front of RALPH.

MAY (*to* EVA): You're splashed. What on earth have you been doing?

RALPH. Only what my mother'd do for me.

MAY. Dry yourself in the scullery.

RALPH *gets out into the towel.*

RALPH. But it's freezing in there.

MAY. Well rub hard.

RALPH *goes.*

TOM. I was here . . . all the time.

MAY. Were you? Yes I can see from the chaos. All these bits Tom.

TOM. Won't take a moment.

He clears up. MAY *inspects the boots.*

MAY. Doesn't he do them nicely? I mean they're just for working in but I'd have had to have thrown them away.

TOM. Should have been stitched. They need some wax round the edges. I'll borrow some off Jack Burndred.

MAY. I'll pay for it.

TOM. He'll lend it. He won't take money.

He looks uneasily at MAY. *But she smiles.*

MAY. Don't be long.

TOM *goes.*

Isn't it good of him, doing that for me? Now . . . what d'you think I've got in the bag?

EVA. What?

MAY. You'll never guess in a million years. A rabbit! The rabbit man was down the market. I haven't seen him in months. It was a miracle he'd got any left.

RALPH *enters rubbing his hair.*

EVA. That's a beauty!

RALPH. He's a big bruiser. By God that's a tasty feller.

MAY. Who said you were having any? Would you skin it
Eva? I don't fancy skinning it.

RALPH. I'll skin it . . . if I can share it. 'Thou shalt not muzzle
the ox that treadeth the corn'.

EVA. Use Tom's knife.

RALPH. I will render it naked as a new born babe.

MAY. How horrible! Take it in there.

RALPH *takes the bag into the scullery.*

EVA. We used to stew ours . . . with apple and anything really.

MAY. Yes. Or we could roast it. Isn't he kind?

EVA. Oh he'll love skinning it, he will . . .

MAY. I meant Tom . . . with the boots. Glad I got something
special. D'you know what I'd do if I could?

EVA. What?

MAY *hesitates.*

MAY. I'd make a stuffing for it. Breadcrumbs and suet. Mince
if I had some. Oh there was a to-do in the market . . . left
me a bit breathless, I think. Never even thought to get a
bunch of parsley.

EVA. Was something happening?

MAY. Just such a crowd, all piling in, buying things. Seemed
like everyone had got Pals on leave. Then suddenly the
clouds come very low, right down to the roof tops . . . and
for three or four minutes there were these huge drops of rain
walloping down and splashing . . . didn't you hear them?

EVA. That's right! I was in the scullery. Big as saucers!

MAY. Yes! And so icy cold. We all run under the tarpaulins
for shelter, shouting and laughing like a lot of kids. People

got talking to one another. They'd got sons home or brothers or husbands. Or sweethearts. And I don't know whether it was the crush or the rain drumming on the sheets . . . but I got quite dizzy. I thought: where am I in all this? Where do I stand . . . to him?

RALPH (*off*): Shall I put it in the big pan or what?

MAY. Get him the meat tin.

EVA *finds the meat tin and goes out briefly.*

EVA (*off*): Put it in this.

RALPH (*off*): D'you want the head? (*Makes a scary noise.*) Whaaaa!

EVA (*off*): Get on with it!

EVA *returns holding a little pan.* MAY *has remained stock still.*

MAY. What's that?

EVA. The head.

MAY *glances at the contents of the pan and screws her face up.*

MAY. Put it over there! I shall have to resolve this, Eva, or I shall burst. My mind goes round and round. I find myself annoyed that I can't cope. I'm not used to it. What does he think of me?

EVA. He loves you.

MAY. No!!

EVA. Yes!

MAY. He thinks I'm mean and a money grubber and we're always at loggerheads over one thing or another.

EVA. You're the apple of Tom's eye! Ralph says so.

MAY. Does he talk about me at camp?

EVA. He gets teased about you.

MAY. Yes . . . about me being a Tartar . . .

EVA. No. They think you'd be quite a catch.

MAY. Oh do they! I suppose they think I'm worth a fortune. Well . . . how do I approach it? Come on. What do I say? Shall I wait till you and Ralph have gone up and then I could say: It's too cold in the parlour for you. You're to come in with me.

EVA. Well, he couldn't resist that, could he?

MAY. Isn't it stupid to be in such an agony about it. And Eva . . . I'm such a novice . . . at my age! Will that make it difficult d'you think?

EVA. I don't know do I?

MAY. You could try and remember! Oh, I'm so glad I've spoken! I will not be a prude, Eva. Cast care to the winds, that's what we must do now.

RALPH *enters with the meat tin and skinned rabbit.*

RALPH. There he is. What'd go nice is some carrots and dumplings.

MAY. Carrots and dumplings would be wonderful!

She pats RALPH's *cheek.*

EVA. Let's splash out. I'll go down for some mince. They'll still be open . . .

MAY. Good idea. You stay. I'll go. I feel like a bit of a run!

Enter TOM *running with* REGGIE *in his arms.* REGGIE *is streaming blood from the nose.*

TOM. Heyup! Out of the road. Give us a hand Ralph. Hold him over the bath!

RALPH *and* TOM *hold the boy so that he bleeds into the bath.*

EVA. Whatever happened?

RALPH. It's a nose bleed.

TOM. Get a cloth! May!

MAY *is stunned.*

I said get a cloth!

EVA. I will . . .

She goes out to the scullery.

REGGIE. Haaa! I'm choking . . .

TOM. Turn his head!

RALPH. They say push a cold key down the back . . .

TOM. Cough it out! Cough!

EVA has returned with a cloth.

EVA (*to* MAY, *indicating cloth*): Will it matter?

MAY shakes her head. EVA wipes REGGIE's face.

TOM. Let him cough a bit more.

RALPH. Aye. Mustn't swaller blood. God isn't it red?

MAY. Can we know what happened?

TOM. He was sitting in the entry next door having a sort of fit. Look at this on his head. What she do Reggie?

REGGIE. Used the strap on me, Mr Hackford.

RALPH. It's the buckle end, that!

EVA. Oh it's deep. Ralph, get clean water.

RALPH goes.

Hold your head back. Look up. That's right. Eh! You don't wear much do you?

She hugs him to her, warming him.

TOM. We'll need the iodine.

MAY. I'd rather you didn't.

RALPH returns with a bowl of water.

RALPH. He's looking better already. Takes more than a clout on the nut don't it Reggie?

REGGIE. Her tried ter hit me agen but I got out!

RALPH. You'll get your Military Medal. Evasion in the face of the enemy.

EVA. Now hold still.

She bathes the cut.

TOM. Should have iodine!

MAY. Let Eva clean it up. Go outwards from it all the way round.

TOM. I've got my field dressing. We'll use that.

MAY. I'd sooner we didn't use anything. If we start bandaging it she'll only think we did it to aggravate her.

MAY stands her ground. TOM and EVA are rebellious. RALPH is embarrassed. EVA tears a little square of cloth and presses it to REGGIE's forehead.

RALPH. That's it love. That'll do the trick.

TOM. He should stay here.

MAY. Whatever are you talking about?

TOM. He's lost blood. He should lie up.

MAY. He can do that at home.

EVA. Why not here?

MAY. It's interfering. He's her son. I'll tell you what we'll do. (*To* REGGIE:) You've got to learn to keep out of trouble, haven't you? I think you go out of your way to get paddled. You've got to realise the war's taken your father away and your mother's that worried. She wants some support from you. Now that's not bleeding any more is it? Keep that little square on, go home and tell your mother I've asked you to start running a few errands for Eva and me on the stall. And for that I have given you an apple (*Gives him one.*) and a threepenny joey. Eat the apple later. Not now for you may have swallowed blood and that'll make you sick. But make sure you show your mother the threepence.

REGGIE. What shall you want me to do?

MAY. Do? There's no end to do. Show it her. Tell her I'll be round tomorrow to ask if it's all right. You understand?

REGGIE. Yes Miss Hassal!

He goes.

RALPH. Clever woman! Eh? Brains!

MAY. It's nothing clever. I just think it's more sensible than inviting trouble.

TOM *moves suddenly. He puts on his tunic followed by his greatcoat.*

Tom, he's only four doors away. He can walk on his own!

He dashes out and returns immediately with his kit bag, stuffing things in.

EVA. What are you doing?

TOM. They're stuck! Stuck! That's why everything's cockeyed. Stuck in their own little worlds. They can't see further than what they know. Mentally stuck. It's got that they think they'll go under for stepping beyond their own back yard.

RALPH. Who's this Tom?

MAY. He means me. When he says 'they' he means me.

TOM. No I don't. I'm talking of the general, not the particular. That's the trouble. They can't generalise. They have to bring everything down to the particular. If you try and explain the theory of the free exchange of skills they think you're talking Chinese! It's the same in a trade. They take on an apprentice and then tell him nowt. Scared stiff of anyone stepping over the line. Scared of imparting knowledge. Well, now they're worried. This war has got them worried. They're cornered. It can't be carried on without the free exchange, d'you see? Skills have got to be taught. It's all out in the open. And the dunderheads and numbskulls that lord it over here, they'll be seen for what they are over there!

MAY. Yes I expect it'll be wonderful over there. Heaven on earth for you. Why do you come here to turn on me and turn on me and go on at me? If that's where you want to be, go there. Get out of my sight.

TOM *hovers uncertainly, then grabs his kit.*

TOM. Ralph can wax the boots. He knows how.

TOM *goes.*

EVA. May, don't let him!

MAY. He has to challenge me . . .

EVA. Stop him Ralph.

RALPH. I'm blowed if I know what it's all about!

EVA. Put your coat on May. I'll get it.

She brings MAY's *coat.*

MAY. If he hadn't challenged me . . .

EVA. He'll be standing in the street wondering what to
do . . .

MAY *allows her to put the coat on her.*

MAY. It isn't as though it comes from him . . . half of it's out
of books! Or from other people. He thinks more of other
people than he does of me! I've been behaving like a
ninny . . .

EVA. Go after him.

MAY. There's not an inch of common ground between us!

EVA. Bring him back. Please!

MAY *goes, hopelessly.*

RALPH. Well it's put me in a right fog. I'm in pea soup here.

Suddenly EVA *goes to him, kissing him on the mouth, the
eyes, all over his face, crushing herself to him.*

Eh little Venus. What's this for?

EVA *breaks away.*

EVA (*indicating the bath*): Help me get this in the yard and
tip it. I'm sure there's enough blood and water and mess
round here.

As they take out the bath, the lights fade.

Scene Ten

A light on MAY *at the stall, now closed up. She stands uncertain what to do. Thinking* TOM *might still be close she whispers:*

MAY. Tom . . . are you there?

> *She senses a movement to one side.*

> Tom!

> CSM RIVERS *enters, muffled up in his greatcoat.*

> Who is it?

RIVERS. Rivers, Miss Hassal. CSM Rivers.

MAY. You should say who you are in the dark!

RIVERS. I'm sorry. No intention to startle you. I was just taking a turn round the streets, saying goodbye to my family . . . or 'adopted' family, I should say, since I've none of my own. That's my fancy, you see. Having taken so many of your menfolk under my wing, I like to think of their kin as mine. Well, he should make the Manchester train easy enough . . .

MAY. Who?

RIVERS. Private Hackford. I saw him on his way just now.

> MAY *is caught unprepared for this.*

> Shine on Accrington! They can talk of duty and service to at GHQ. They should come and see this. There's people here don't talk of it . . . they *know*. They've faced the worst that could come with no defence, no cushioning, nothing but wearing out the way to work and back on long hours and short commons. People who've faced death already for their nearest and dearest . . . and felt it coming round the corner and stood up to it one road or the other. But that's the valour of life and there's no medals for it. I don't know what those Prussians and Saxons and Woortenburgers think they've got behind them to stand against this!

MAY. He wanted the Pals and he's got the Pals.

She goes. RIVERS *remains. As the light fades we hear,
distantly, a low rumble of guns and machine gun fire.*

ACT TWO

Scene One

The sound of machine guns, distant.

   RALPH *and* EVA *are revealed.* RALPH *is in France. He is in full service marching order, exhausted from marching, leaning against the tarpaulin.* EVA *sits, quietly tacking the hem of a white muslin dress by lamplight in* MAY's *kitchen.*

RALPH. Oh my dearest, my own little pocket Venus . . . my rose of Clayton-le-Moors. This is no letter you'll ever get. My love. Sweet Eva. It's come. After God's long ages it's come and we're up to the line for the big push. But for the moment we're lost, as ever. Lost three times finding support trench. Now lost again. It's like a bake oven this summer night. I'm in a muck sweat. My sore throat's back. I've spewed my ring up twice. They say Jerry's beat but there's lads seen his observer balloons up all afternoon watching every move we made. I was ready enough once. Christmas when they sent us off to fuckin Egypt to fight Johnnie Turk. But he was whipped before we got there so I'd got myself ready for nowt. I was ready when they brought us back and into France. But it's been up and down, round and round, in and out, waiting and waiting till I don't know how I shall go at it. I've heard the flies buzzing out there. Every shell or bomb as falls short sends up clouds. Still, they're only old regulars lying out there, who, as May would say, are very low at the best of times. I've been a bastard to you Eva, if you only knew. Slept with whores. And one little mam'selle in Amiens who'd take no pay. I sat on her doorstep right after and cried for you. All I want to

volunteer for now is a night raid on your bosom in a field
of snowy white bedsheets. That's a fact.

The light on RALPH *fades. There is more light on* EVA *who
begins to work on the dress with a sewing machine. The
sound of the sewing machine rises above the fading away of
the machine guns.* MAY *enters.*

MAY. Oh you've not!

EVA. It's not much . . .

MAY. But I said I'd do it. For I know it goes against the grain.
Still you're better with the machine than yours truly. It is
not my forté. I shouldn't have worn this, it was too hot for
me. (*Removes coat.*) And I think I've torn it under the arm.
Am I getting fat?

EVA. You? Hardly.

MAY. There's a bit more than there was in the basement area.
And Mrs Dickenson had such a lovely summer jacket in
nigger-brown velvet with little tufts of squirrel here and
here. I felt right outfaced as usual. How's the tea?

EVA. A bit old.

MAY. It'll do. They're all looking forward to hearing you.

EVA. Are they? Ooo . . . er!

MAY. You'll be the prize attraction. And if this weather holds
it will be so glorious. Her garden! Such immaculate lawns. It
makes you wonder what you're living for. Such blooms!

EVA. Did you take Reggie in?

MAY. Now there I've got a confession. My courage failed me.
I left him down the road in the park and carried the baskets
myself. Isn't that dreadful? And I got a shock when I got
back to him. There he was flat out on the grass. I thought
he's had another do. But no . . . he was right as rain. I
said: 'What's the matter . . . are you tired?' He says: 'No
miss, I'm listening for the guns!'

EVA. Oh they all think that. Some put their ears to the
railway lines.

MAY. The guns in France? He says there's been freak hearings in Yorkshire . . . I says I'm not surprised. Are you finished?

EVA. Just a bit round the sleeve.

MAY. And I'll do the sash.

She gets needle and thread and a red, white and blue sash to sew.

The sunset was an absolute picture. I was standing gawping at it at the end of the street when up comes Sarah. She said you and she and Bertha were going to the Red Lion.

EVA. Oh yes. Yes we are.

MAY. No you're not.

EVA. What did you say?

MAY. You look as if you could murder me you do. I know you know what I think. And I know you think I don't know what goes these days. I said to Sarah: 'Get a jug and one for me and come round here.'

EVA. Here? You didn't!

MAY. Why not? Go to the pub and you're only on sufferance. You're either with the drabs or the fancy women. And Sarah's you can't go to for her mother being a misery all over . . . and Bertha's brothers are pure purgatory. What are you staring at?

EVA. You and your hen party.

MAY. I'm not that inflexible you know. Anyway, I feel a bit like celebrating. Put the dress on. Let's see how it hangs.

EVA. Celebrating what?

MAY. Well . . . the war ending.

EVA. Oh yes. One more push.

MAY. Put it on.

MAY helps her as she removes her own dress and puts the other on. Then MAY hugs her.

EVA. Oh you are in a mood!

MAY. I shall have to tell you. I've found the shop. The shop I've been looking for. Did you think I'd given up the idea. I've found it and it's beautiful.

EVA. Where?

MAY. Somerset Road, if you know it. Across the park on the other side. I haven't let on about it in case it was another dead-end place. But it's perfection. High-class provision store. Calls itself an emporium but it's not too big and it's very reasonable. The man who ran it has gone to the Manchesters and his wife can't cope.

EVA. Have you taken it?

MAY. Not yet. I've still to decide finally. The house has a hot water system. Back boiler! There's a proper bath and a tiled range and a little bit of a real garden with a hedge.

EVA. It sounds marvellous. It is exactly what you wanted isn't it? I'm so happy for you.

MAY. For me?

EVA. I can easily move in with the Henshalls next to Bertha's.

MAY. Oh no! No. I want you to come in with me.

EVA. Well. It's a bit far.

MAY. From here? Of course it is.

EVA. I meant from work.

MAY. Haven't I made it clear? I want you to come in with me. As a partner. Leave the mill. You won't need that anymore.

EVA. What d'you mean?

MAY. Share it. Live there. Divide the profits. Or pool all together. However you wish.

EVA. But I should need some money, shouldn't I?

MAY. I've thought of that. We pay the rent from the takings . . . and for the stock and so forth, I'll lend you half and you can repay as we go, a little at a time.

EVA. I'm a dunce at money.

MAY. You are not a dunce at anything.

EVA. A bit of a wrench. I've made so many friends.

MAY. They can come and see us . . . from time to time.
Mrs Dickenson has given her word she'll patronise it. Some
of her neighbours do already. We'll have a delivery boy with
a bike.

EVA. Reggie'll like that.

MAY. Oh yes. Though give him a bike and it'd disappear in a
puff of smoke. There's a copper beech tree just beyond the
garden and I can see the sun shining on it and the rain falling
on it and the snow . . . such Christmasses we could have . . .

EVA. Aren't you good? Aren't you very, very good?

MAY. Oh I'm not out for goodness but an end to all these dark
streets and rows and argie-bargies and niggling over tick and
farthings off. There are more things in heaven and earth
Horatio . . . Put on the sash Madam and I'll get the things.

She goes off. Slowly EVA *puts on the red, white and blue
sash.* MAY *returns with a cardboard Union Jack shield and a
cardboard Britannia helmet and trident.*

Right. Hold your toasting fork! Other hand! Look dignified.

EVA. They'll be saying: Fancy her! Listen to that twang!

MAY. You have not got a twang. And you will sing like Madam
Patti.

EVA. More like Clara Butterknickers.

MAY. Please! This is the Tipparary Club . . . raising funds for
our gallant boys. Oh there was a nasty moment apparently.
One of the ladies on the organising committee looked down
the programme and saw that you were singing 'Oh Peaceful
England' by Edward German. She says: 'Oh dear I don't
think we should print that word' Mrs Dickenson says:
'What word?' She says: 'German!' Well you know Mrs
Dickenson. She stood right up and said: 'That is an uncalled
for slight on one of this country's most honoured
musicians. Mr German is as English as roast beef'.

EVA. So I'm still singing it?

MAY. Of course you are. Stupid woman saying that.

EVA. Haven't you forgotten Tom?

MAY. Tom?

EVA. Well . . . you and me, sharing a shop. What about Tom?

MAY. What about Tom?

EVA. Say something about him . . .

MAY. What should I say that isn't obvious? He's gone his way.
And I'm relieved he has. I'm enjoying life as I haven't for
years. And that's due to you. Not Tom. We can do as we like.
Get our meals as we like. I can get something for you . . . you
can get something for me just as the mood takes us. We're
not forever treading on eggshells, being touchy, afraid to
speak are we?

EVA *takes off the things and gets out of the dress.*

EVA. I don't think you're being honest. I don't think that's
what you really feel at all. And I think you've forgotten
that when Ralph comes back if he still wants to I shall marry
him.

MAY. Now what's this? I won't have you saying I'm not honest.

EVA. So is it that you want to get into this shop because you
think the war's going to be over and the girls'll have nothing
to spend anymore?

MAY. I should not let myself be questioned by anyone else but
you. But I'll admit there is something of that to it, yes.

EVA. And will you say that you want me there because if I'm
there then Ralph may come there and if Ralph comes there
then Tom may come too.

MAY. If you think that I don't want you for yourself and
your company then I'm sorry. And if you think that I still
want him dogging me and tugging at me and not letting me
go . . . leaving me alone to do what I so much wish to do . . .
then I'm hurt by that. You have hurt me!

Blackout. The sound of artillery barrage.

Scene Two

*MAY sits at the table, a little time later, doing her accounts.
She will not be able to concentrate on them for her own thoughts
crowding in.*

   *Meanwhile the lights are brought up on TOM in full kit
standing by the tarpaulin. The sound of the guns has continued.
The letter he speaks is one she will not get till later. She must
never seem to react to it in any way. But, of course, his presence
in her mind is very strong.*

TOM. Dear May, just a few lines to thank you for the parcel. I
   hardly know what to say, it was so generous, all things
   considered. It bought you many good opinions of Ralph
   and Arthur and the rest, and not least of me. I hope you don't
   mind me sharing it as we do all parcels here. There was much
   praise for the kidney soup and strawberry jam, a most welcome
   change from our endless Maconochie and plum and apple. In
   return I hope to send you the sketches I've done here of
   various Pals you will recognise. What I have tried to capture
   in their faces is that free spirit of comradeship you see out
   here but never see at home. Despite the rough life it's the
   best feeling on earth the way we're all for one and one for
   each. And that's lesson number one for when this is over
   if we're not to go back to the old narrow ways they force
   on us. I still have the snapshots of you and will use my best
   endeavours to render your portrait in crayon, though it
   can never live up to the good heart and splendid appearance
   of the original. Yours in gratitude and affection, Tom.

*The light on TOM fades. He goes off.
MAY puts her accounts away. Suddenly the gunfire ceases.
The lights go up in the kitchen area for:*

Scene Three

Half an hour later. SARAH *and* BERTHA *dance into the kitchen singing at the tops of their voices.* MAY *has changed mood. She claps her hands in time to the singing but her mood is somewhat forced.* EVA *appears, pouring beer from a jug into a mug.*

EVA. Shall you have some more?

MAY. Of course I shall! Shall I have some more! Pour it out!

BERTHA. Ooh! I do wish you'd stop feeling!

   She has broken away from SARAH.

SARAH. You what?

BERTHA. You know!

MAY. Sarah! What are you doing?

SARAH. Well I've got to cuddle something somehow.

BERTHA. You are becoming awful.

MAY. I think you want a bucket of water over you.

EVA. Shall I fill one up?

SARAH. It wouldn't douse me. It's your fault Bertha. You look quite the little man in that uniform.

BERTHA. I don't!

EVA. Someone doesn't think so . . .

   Pause. They look at BERTHA.

SARAH. Who?

BERTHA. It's nobody . . .

SARAH. She's got a masher!

BERTHA. I haven't!

MAY. You've found a young man?

BERTHA. No!

EVA. He's an electrician.

SARAH. You've got an electrician? They earn a fortune! Where d'you find him?

BERTHA. On the tram. He works on the trams. Comes out to us and does the wires . . . you know. Well he rides on the platform sometimes. Doesn't really say anything.

SARAH. Too busy watching you go upstairs, you little goof.

MAY. Don't be so foul.

EVA. She's only jealous. He's proposed.

MAY. Really?

SARAH. Never!

BERTHA. No he hasn't! At first I thought he was a bit gormless. Although you have to be clever to do his job, I know. But he'd just stand there grinning . . . with his mouth half open, like this. I thought, Oh lor, I wish he'd go away.

SARAH. Get on to the proposal . . .

BERTHA. It wasn't. He just suddenly said in a very loud voice, 'Are you the marrying kind?' I said: 'Are you speaking to me?' He said, 'Well I'm not speaking to her.' And that was so embarrassing because two seats away there was a nun. Well you know nuns when they've got their back to you, you never know what they're thinking.

SARAH. What did you say?

BERTHA. Oh I said, 'I wouldn't marry you if you were the last person on earth.'

SARAH. Good. That'll keep him guessing.

MAY. He isn't one of these who wants to marry to avoid the conscription is he?

EVA. No, that's the thing. He can't pass the medical. He has asthma.

MAY. My goodness, I should think about it Bertha. Electricians with asthma don't grow on trees!

BERTHA *sniffs and blows her nose.*

EVA. May . . . you've upset her.

MAY. What have I said?

EVA. She doesn't want to think of it that way.

MAY. Oh? Are we so sensitive?

EVA. Yes we are! She's had an offer and she doesn't want it. Isn't that enough to upset anyone?

BERTHA. Even if I liked him more I couldn't love him. I couldn't love a man who'd stayed at home . . .

MAY. It's not his fault . . .

BERTHA. That makes it worse. If he was a dodger I could tell him straight. How could I face father? Say he was wounded or gassed . . . how could I? ✶

SARAH. Come on! There's half this jug left. I'm not having it go flat. Drink it up. They'll soon be back. You've read what the guns have done. The Germans are blown to smithereens. Buried alive in their dugouts. There'll be none left to fight. The Pals'll be marching through the town and we'll be cheering . . . and I shall have Bill back picking his nose and spitting in the fire and breaking wind fit to blow the ornaments off the what not.

MAY. Sarah! You're in my kitchen.

SARAH. Well it isn't holy ground . . . is it Eva? Yes I fancied one of those tall bronzed Australians or Canadians but there you are. And what about Ralph. Eh Bertha . . . eh? Back to Eva's loving arms. Oh Eva! Is he masterful? Is he passionate? Is he wild?

EVA. I sometimes think I'm the one that's wild. He can be very gentle.

SARAH. Not Bill. He's a steam-hammer. If he missed me he'd have the bedroom wall down! I used to get weary of being pulverised but I wouldn't mind now. Here's to loved ones!

EVA.
BERTHA. } Loved ones!

MAY. Love!

EVA. Yes. Love.

MAY. You talk about love?

EVA. Yes!

MAY. It's all so sordid. So bestial!

EVA. Don't you say that!

MAY. I shall. I shall. I don't care what you think of me for it.
I don't. Oh no . . . not you, Eva. I don't mean you. I envy
you. You just sail right through it. It doesn't seem to affect
you.

EVA. What doesn't?

MAY. This mean, dirty foul-mouthed place.

SARAH. I see . . .

MAY. Where's love round here? Men round here . . . ignorant,
stoney-faced callous oafs, sitting in the best chair waiting
to be fed, like overgrown babies. Big fat cuckoos in the nest.
I'll tell you what love is to them.

EVA. Some are different.

MAY. Some? Yes, there's the silly and stupid side of it. You so
hope there's someone who'll rise above it that you're ready
to deceive yourself over fools . . . thinking other people are
what they're not and never will be. There's just everything to
be done before you can even think of love. Oh God I'm
drunk. I'm drunk! Drunk! I shall put this aside, Sarah, thank
you very much . . . and I shall go to bed. Goodnight,
goodnight, goodnight.

She goes.

SARAH. You'll have to do something. You'll have to part.

BERTHA. I feel a bit sick.

SARAH (*to* BERTHA): Come on. Fresh air. (*To* EVA:) You'd
be very well liked round here if it wasn't for that one. D'you
know? Move out. Don't tell her. Just move out.

EVA. I can't. Not just yet anyway.

SARAH. Oh not that bloody Tipperary concert. Don't show up.

EVA. I must. If I didn't . . . I don't know what she'd do.

Blackout as they go.

Scene Four

Western Front, the Somme. The height of the artillery barrage.
Flashes in the darkness. Against the tarpaulin we see TOM,
RALPH and ARTHUR crouched down in full kit, trying to stop
the noise from their ears. The stage begins to lighten. Suddenly
the barrage stops. We hear the birds singing. TOM and RALPH
rise slowly. ARTHUR remains in some kind of trance.
Now we hear occasional bursts of fire from the German guns.

RALPH. Not in daylight! Not in bloody daylight! Why leave it
    so late? We could have gone over in the dark. They'll see us
    all now!

VOICE (*off*): Stand by!

VOICE (*off*): Close up Nine Platoon! Iggery, iggery!

TOM. Every man should have two jobs.

RALPH. Hitch my big pack up Tom . . .

TOM (*hitching the pack as RALPH loosens straps*): No one
    should be stuck forever in one boring job. We should all share
    the tedious work and the interesting work.

RALPH. Fuck! I've broke this nail. Loose this strap will you?

    TOM *does so.*

    If I'm in a shell hole I'm going to be out of this like greased
    shit. The water in them holes can drown you.

TOM. It needs thinkers in charge, not thick heads. Rational
    men. Men who have proper regard for the thoughts of others.
    Readers. Men who've taken the trouble to read what the
    thinkers have to say.

RALPH. I'm not going to drown. Shot or blown to bits but not
    drowned. Loose your straps. I reckon if you're out of your
    pack quick enough and get it under your feet you might keep
    up. But tie your water bottle separate. Fuck all use not
    drowning if you die of thirst! Oh these straps. I'll never get
    out fast enough.

TOM. You could cut them.

RALPH. I've tried. Bayonet's too blunt!

TOM. Borrow this.

RALPH. That's your leather knife . . . What will you do?

TOM. Oh aye . . .

RALPH. What you made of Tom? You going over there to talk philosophy with them?

TOM. There's a lot of good German philosophers.

RALPH. Well there's fuck-all of them over there! Wake up Arthur, get up.

VOICE (*off*): Move up nine platoon. Move!

ARTHUR (*to his pet pigeon England's Glory*): Now sweet . . . now my beauty . . . the sun is shining and the air is clear . . .

RALPH. Hold on to me Tom. Oh mother, I've got the movies. Push me if you see me falling back . . . don't let them see me go back. Christ I'm clasped so tight I'll bust!

CSM RIVERS *dashes in to join them.*

RIVERS. Heads down! Get your heads down! Seven-thirty ack-emma . . . mines detonating.

VOICES. Stand by! Stand by! Take cover!

RIVERS. Brace yourselves!

A vast deep roaring sound as the Hawthornden Ridge mine goes off. They cower and sway as the shock waves go through the trench.

Well the Pals! Next stop Serre for Beaumont Hamel, Bapaume and Berlin! (*Shouts off.*) Mr Williams, sir! Move your platoon up! (*Quietly to* TOM:) Think of her, shall we Hackford . . . think of her? If you lose your officers don't make for the gaps in the wire . . . Jerry's got his Spandaus trained on the gaps and he'll rip you to pieces . . . cut your own; understood? Got your wire cutters?

TOM. Yes sir.

RIVERS. Let glory shine from your arseholes today boys. Rise on the whistle . . . dress from the right . . . rifles at the port

. . . go steady and we'll be drinking schnappes and eating
sausages by sundown. Boggis . . . let's have a prayer.

ARTHUR. Oh God . . . do you smile still? Do you smile to see
your handiwork?

*Whistles begin to blow around the theatre, merging into
one another.*

RIVERS. Over we go . . . stay in line . . . right marker!

VOICES. Come on the Pals. Up the Accringtons! Nine platoon!
Ten platoon! With me, with me, with me! Dress from the
right. Leave that man! Leave him!

They go over the top.
*Mingling with the machine guns stuttering we hear an
awkward, heavy piano introduction to Edward German's
'Oh Peaceful England' being played.*
EVA *appears in her Brittania costume. She is singing at the
fund raising concert. She looks tense and nervous . . . almost
angry. She begins to sing:*

EVA (*sings*):
Oh peaceful England, while I my watch am keeping,
Thou like Minerva weary of war art sleeping.
Sleep on a little while and in thy slumber smile.
While thou art sleeping I my watch am keeping.
Sword and buckler by thy side, rest on the shore of battle-
tide,
Which like the ever hungry sea, howls round this Isle.
Sleep till I awaken thee, and in thy slumber smile.
England, fair England, well hast thou earned thy slumber,
Yet though thy bosom no breast-plate now encumber . . .

*Suddenly she breaks off. She's lost the next line. The
accompanyist falters.* EVA *begins to shake with fury at the
situation she's put herself in. She exclaims something and
runs off.*

Scene Five

SARAH HARDING's *back yard. She is pegging out washing. Off-stage* ANNIE *calls for her son. She gives the customary low note on the first syllable, followed by a long drawn out falsetto scream on the second:*

ANNIE (*off*): Re-hhh-gggeeee! Re-hhh-gggeeee!

> *She enters and repeats the cry. She is in her own back yard next door.*

SARAH. Oh please Annie don't . . . please don't . . .

ANNIE. He's not hiding in your yard is he?

SARAH. No. He isn't.

ANNIE. I bet he is.

SARAH. I tell you he isn't.

ANNIE. He'd better show himself quick. I want him!

SARAH. Yes, I heard you say so. Well I haven't seen him.

ANNIE. Right. Re-hhh-gggeeee!

SARAH. Oh come on round and look if you're that suspicious.

ANNIE. I'll take your word for it . . .

SARAH. Come round! Back gate's open . . . come and look.

> ANNIE *moves round to her. She looks in vain.*

ANNIE. Well where is he then?

SARAH. I don't know. Is he with Eva at the stall?

ANNIE. Eeeee-vvaahhhh!

SARAH. Give over! My head's like suet pudding.

ANNIE. And whose fault is that?

SARAH. That beer was off. I swear it was. It looked a bit cloudy from the start. He's no right serving it in that condition. I feel like my father when mother used to say: 'put your head under the tap, Bernard, your eyes are like piss-holes in the snow'.

REGGIE *sneaks quietly on stage, sidling towards safety.*

ANNIE. There! There you are! Come round here. Come into Mrs Harding's.

SARAH. Annie, I've got to do this . . .

ANNIE. It won't take a moment. Come on. I'll not keep telling you . . .

REGGIE *moves a little closer.*

Yes, I'm not surprised you keep your distance you devil! The bobby's been at the door. Bobby Machin's been round for you. They'll have you in the cells . . . locked up in the dark with nowt to eat . . . they will!

SARAH. What's he done then?

ANNIE. He was caught learning a gang of the little ones how to fish in the canal.

SARAH. Is that all? I'm astonished Bobby Machin said a word then. If he catches them he usually passes his helmet round for ha'pennies.

ANNIE. I'm trying to learn him to act right! Anyway it wasn't all . . . was it you filthy animal? See . . . he thought I wouldn't know the rest. Bobby Machin told me. He was getting those little children . . . those little nine year olds . . . oooh you beast . . . getting them to repeat a rhyme after him. Look at him. He knows what I'm talking about.

SARAH. Surely it's not the end of the world . . .

ANNIE. You can hear it. Because he's going to say it. He's going to stand there till he's said it out loud. You dirty-minded mongrel . . . you're going to say it in front of Mrs Harding, now!

SARAH. I'm sure I don't want to listen . . .

ANNIE. And just the first bit . . . d'you hear? Just the first bit. Say it. Say it.

REGGIE (*mumbles*): I wish I was a little mouse . . .

ANNIE. Louder!

REGGIE. I wish I was a little mouse . . .

ANNIE. And the next bit . . .

REGGIE. To run up mother's clothes . . .

ANNIE. That's it! No more!

REGGIE. And see the hairy tunnel . . .

ANNIE. Enough!

REGGIE. Where dadder's chuff-chuff goes!

She runs at him to take a swipe but REGGIE *is off.*

ANNIE. I said enough! (*To* SARAH:) I only meant you to hear the first bit. (*After* REGGIE:) You wait! You wait!

SARAH. It's a long time since I heard that one.

ANNIE. You've heard it?

SARAH. And so have you.

ANNIE. I have never listened to that sort of thing in my life!

SARAH. Haven't you? I used to wring it out of my brothers. All them songs they used to start off and not finish. I used to shut them in the bedroom till they told me.

ANNIE. Oh what I have to contend with! And if Arthur was here all he'd say is: 'Follow Jesus' What good's that to kids?

SARAH. Well, if we all followed Jesus we wouldn't have any kids.

ANNIE. What?

SARAH. He didn't did he? None that they mention in the Bible anyway.

ANNIE *is shocked but has to laugh.*

That's better.

ANNIE. Only you could say that!

SARAH. I dare the thunderbolt I do.

ANNIE. If I'd known what was going to happen in my life. I know what people think about me. I'm weary. I'm weary of it all.

BERTHA *runs on with a copy of The Accrington Observer.*

BERTHA. It's here! It's over! We've won!

SARAH. Won what?

BERTHA. The war! (*Calls off:*) Eva! May! We've won! I've got the paper. We're through the lines!

SARAH. Read it.

BERTHA. 'British offensive . . .' No, I can't. I'll just shout to my mother and get May and Eva . . .

She runs off shouting.

(*Off:*) May! Eve! Is my mother there?

ANNIE: What's it say?

SARAH. 'British offensive begins. Official. Front line broken over sixteen miles'. Oh Jesus forgive me!

Enter MAY and EVA.

MAY. Is it over? Just tell me if it's over . . .

SARAH. The German's are running . . .

EVA. Read it!

SARAH. I'm trying . . . 'Front line broken over sixteen miles. The push that could end the war has now been launched. British and Empire infantry are now in possession of German trenches, their exhausted occupants decimated by continuous shellfire over the past weeks. Those not killed are falling back in disorder as our victorious troops press home their advantage.'

BERTHA *returns breathless.*

BERTHA. Didn't I tell you . . .

MAY. Read it!

ANNIE. Does it mention the Pals?

SARAH. You read it Eva . . .

ANNIE. Are the Pals in it?

EVA. 'Preceded by a bombardment of an hour and a half

such as Armageddon had never seen' . . . Nothing about the
Pals yet . . . (*Opens paper.*) Ah! 'Some of the battalions
opened their advance by kicking a football ahead of them.
They went over cheering as at a cup-final' . . . no . . . no . . .
'Censorship will not allow the actual units to be named' . . .
they won't say.

BERTHA. We're through! We're through!

MAY. Is there more?

EVA. Only a handful of the German machine gunners were
left to man their posts. Fire was wild and panic-stricken,
though, inevitably, some of our brave soldiers fell . . . here
and there . . . refusing help and urging their comrades on'.

ANNIE. They don't say any more?

EVA. No. No details. Or names.

BERTHA. I don't know where mother's got to. Oh what a
relief . . . after all this time!

MAY (*to* EVA): Let me have it please.

ANNIE. He'll not have had the sense to keep out of it. His
back could have kept him out.

SARAH. Come on Annie . . . it's victory! 'God save our gracious
King'.

BERTHA. Hurrah!

SARAH. I'm glad I put the flags out . . .

She holds a pair of drawers against her.

Up the Pals!

ANNIE. Yes. That's your flag, that is!

SARAH. Well . . . there's a few battles been fought under it
I admit! I've got a little drop of gin hidden in the scullery.
I'll get it.

She hands the drawers to EVA *and goes.*

Peg 'em up for me love.

MAY. 'More detailed information will become available in the next few days . . .'

BERTHA. I thank God. I thank Thee God . . .

EVA. Could you hand me a peg?

BERTHA. Oh yes.

ANNIE. I wouldn't touch her bloomers with a barge pole.

BERTHA. What's the matter Eva?

EVA. Thinking.

SARAH *returns with the gin.*

SARAH. Shall I pass it round?

ANNIE. No thanks.

EVA *and* BERTHA *share it.* MAY *shakes her head as she leafs through the paper.*

SARAH. The Pals . . .

MAY. Oh there's a paragraph about the concert.

EVA. I don't want to hear it.

MAY. I'm going to read it.

EVA. No.

MAY. But it's wonderful! 'It was a great emotional climax to the evening when Eva Mason as Britannia rendered Edward German's *Oh Peaceful England* with such purity and nobility of tone . . . and it was surely fitting that the singer herself was so overcome that she was unable to complete the final lines of the song. This spontaneous demonstration of true feeling left no eye unassailed by tears!'

SARAH. I thought you said you'd forgot the bloody words!

EVA. I had!

MAY. Never mind. You triumphed.

BERTHA. Isn't that funny?

EVA. So much for papers!

During this, at some point, ANNIE *has spotted something offstage that holds her attention.*

ANNIE. What's that over there . . .

SARAH. Are you mentioned May?

MAY. Yes, I'm listed amongst the helpers, next to Mrs Henry.

SARAH. Oooer!

ANNIE. That bird. Will you look at it Sarah?

SARAH. Where?

ANNIE. On our coal house roof.

SARAH. I can't see anything . . .

BERTHA. Oooh. My head's in such a whirl . . .

ANNIE. Shut up! It's coming back over the ridge. There with it's wing hanging down . . .

SARAH. That pigeon?

ANNIE. It's come back.

MAY. What are you talking about?

ANNIE. D'you think I don't recognise it? It's come to the coop.

SARAH. You haven't got any pigeons . . .

ANNIE. It's his! It's England's Glory.

SARAH. Don't be daft!

MAY. What is it?

SARAH. She thinks it's the bird Arthur took to France. It can't possibly be!

ANNIE. See. It's dragging one wing. Oh God! It's got blood on it!

BERTHA. No. It couldn't have flown all this way . . .

EVA. Oh surely you're mistaken . . .

ANNIE. I'm not. It's finding its perch.

SARAH. It's one of George Deakin's. They're always round pecking for bits. Ugh! I can't stand feathers . . . them thin little bodies all puffed out . . . Shooo!

ANNIE. Don't! It'll go into coop.

They all watch fascinated, catching ANNIE's *mood. Suddenly they start back.* SARAH *screams.*

SARAH. I'm not going to look . . .

BERTHA. It'll fall . . .

EVA. It's half dead . . .

MAY. What's it doing, edging down the roof like that?

ANNIE. It's England's Glory. I daren't put a foot in there. Will one of you get it?

SARAH. Oh Lord. No!

ANNIE. One of you go.

MAY. Whatever for?

ANNIE. See if there's anything with it. If there's a thing on its leg.

EVA. I'll go. I'm used to birds. Can I take your bucket, Sarah?

SARAH. What for?

EVA. To put it in.

SARAH. No! Oh all right.

EVA *goes off with the bucket.*

MAY. It's just some stray that a cat's worried and let go of . . .

ANNIE. Tell her there's a sack in the coop. She can cover it over with . . .

BERTHA. Eva. Cover it with the sack out of the coop!

MAY. You mustn't give way to imaginings.

ANNIE. Don't tell me I'm imagining! I felt it would come many a time. I've laid awake thinking I'd see it in the morning.

BERTHA (*calls*): Be careful!

SARAH. Oh my stomach!

BERTHA. She can hardly reach it . . .

SARAH. Eva . . . don't! Don't let her bring it in!

SARAH *retreats as* EVA *enters nursing the bucket with the sack over it.*

EVA. It's an awful mess . . .

SARAH. Keep it under! Don't let it get out . . .

EVA. It's dying . . .

ANNIE. Never mind that. What's it brought?

EVA. Nothing . . .

ANNIE. Its leg. On its leg!

EVA. Just a clip . . . and a number . . .

ANNIE. Nothing else?

EVA. No. Nothing.

ANNIE. Get rid of it. Burn it. Put it on the fire!

SARAH. Take it away!

EVA. Poor thing. Heart's hardly beating. I'll drown it.

She goes. ANNIE *sways.*

MAY. Sarah . . . get a chair for her.

BERTHA. Mrs Boggis! There wasn't anything.

ANNIE. It's the end for me.

MAY. Talk sense.

ANNIE. It's the last I'll do.

BERTHA. Shall I get smelling salts?

ANNIE. I can't see. Where are you? Are you there or not?

SARAH. Have a little drink of this . . .

ANNIE. No! I'll not drink! I'll not eat . . . I'll not do nowt.

REGGIE *enters quietly, unobserved.*

The fool's dead. So he's dead. I never wanted him in the first place. I would never have had him if that soft half-wit thing hadn't been born and I had to have someone! I'd have never had his. But I'll do nothing for them now. His mother can care for them. Not me. They say I nearly died of scarlet fever when I was four. I wish I had!

She flings herself down, crawling. EVA *enters.*

BERTHA. Oh don't Mrs Boggis, please.

ANNIE. I shall eat stones. I shall eat stones . . . that's what I'll eat now . . .

EVA. Let's get her home.

REGGIE *comes forward.*

REGGIE. I'll do that. Stop staring at her!

ANNIE (*clinging to him*): Oh Reggie. You're the one who's mine.

REGGIE. Stop making a show. Get up. Stop staring!

ANNIE. You won't go will you? You won't go. Where is this? Where is it? What's that wall? There's a brown gate. I don't know any brown gate . . .

REGGIE *helps her off-stage, slowly.*

MAY. Well how silly to let yourself go like that. And say things like that. I always thought she had a bit of sense. As though that bird could have come from France. As though it meant anything if it did.

BERTHA. That's what I think . . .

SARAH. I hate birds . . .

EVA. Let me borrow your little shovel Sarah. I'll go and bury it.

Scene Six

A day later. MAY's kitchen. EVA enters wearing a shawl and carrying a small bag and a bunch of flowers.
She listens for MAY. Silence. She takes a chair and places it carefully and sits staring at a spot on the floor, still holding the flowers.
She thinks of something and her eyes turn towards the kitchen. She lays the flowers on the table and goes off a moment.
She returns, dragging the long tin bath. She places it just where it was when RALPH bathed in it and kneels by it. She reaches out to the invisible form of RALPH in the bath and touches him,

on the shoulders, down the arms, round the chest.
Then, as she sits, staring, slowly fade lights to dim.
After a while MAY enters.

MAY. Oh! You frightened me. Eva? Eva . . .

> *She goes off and returns with the lamp.*

Sitting in the dark?

EVA. It wasn't dark.

MAY. You really mustn't dwell on things that have no
foundation. There's work to do. We have to plan. I've seen
Mr Brownlow in the market. He's interested in the stall for his
niece . . . though he won't agree a price yet. Are you going to
use that bath or what?

> EVA, *furious, drags the bath away to the scullery, off-stage.*
> *Presently she returns.*

MAY. If you're going to lose your temper with me maybe
we'd better not speak. You've changed.

EVA. Yes. I've lost Ralph.

MAY. Oh this is so foolish. I've looked in on Annie. She's had
a temporary relapse. But in moments she has her wits about
her and she's very sorry she's caused anyone to worry. I've
brought you the paper.

EVA. I don't want to see it . . .

MAY. There is absolutely no report of the Pals being in the
advance. The casualties so far are mostly lightly wounded and
very few killed . . .

EVA. They're lying.

MAY. Why should they lie?

EVA. For their own ends . . . I don't know why. They take it on
themselves to decide what we hear about and what we don't.
Haven't we proved it over and over? Go out in the street
and ask. They all believe the Pals were there. Why should you
be the one that doesn't?

MAY. There's no law that says you must go along with the herd!

EVA *moves quickly towards her with her hand raised. She stops herself.*

You'd do that to me? Then you can go as well.

Fade to blackout.

Scene Seven

There are lights on the stall. REGGIE *pushes on the handcart. He is tense and close to tears. He works quickly, undoing the tarpaulin, setting out the baskets.* MAY *appears with her scales and money bag.*

MAY. Now I told you not to come.

REGGIE. Gran's round to put her to bed.

MAY. But it's you your mother needs. I thought she was improving today.

REGGIE. Her started screaming again.

MAY. Oh dear, did she? She must get a good night's sleep.

REGGIE. Her wanted rug out of kitchen burnt. We had to hide it.

MAY. Why?

REGGIE. Her said it was all muddy and bloody.

MAY. Oh what next?

REGGIE. Her thinks her saw Father standing on it. He come in through front door, her says. Stood on rug wi' a big hole here . . . in his neck, dropping blood.

MAY. It's only what she's saying. Take no notice. She'll get over it. He's not dead. We'll mix a few nice things up for her.

Enter BERTHA.

BERTHA. Oh May have you seen Sarah?

MAY. Not since this morning.

BERTHA. I knocked at her door. She wasn't back.

MAY (*to* REGGIE): Take them. Make sure she has her sleeping draught. If you need me shout for me.

REGGIE. Thank you, miss.

He goes.

BERTHA. That's funny. She set out before me. She went to the station. I went to the Town Hall.

MAY. What for?

BERTHA. To see what we could find out.

MAY. Turn that lamp down for me love, or I'll be had up for showing too much light.

BERTHA. There was quite a few at Town Hall, but they said we was to clear off and stop spreading rumour.

MAY. Quite right.

BERTHA. But everyone's going up and down, round and round, they'll go out of their minds. Who's that over there? Sarah? No. All the nurses have been stopped their leave, have you heard? Jessie Bains had only just got home and there was a bobby round at their home with an order for her to go back. She'd only time for a cup of tea and she was back on the train. Listen! There's people shouting down the hill. People running.

SARAH (*off*): Bertha!

BERTHA. Sarah!

SARAH *runs on, white and breathless. During what she says* EVA *will enter quietly, to one side.*

SARAH. Seven . . . seven . . . there's only seven of them left. The Pals. Only seven left alive. Out of nearly seven hundred men.

BERTHA. Oh no God . . . don't . . . don't . . .

SARAH. We talked to the railwaymen that had been at Manchester Central. There's crowds there trying to find out what they can from the drivers and people coming from London. Well apparently it's certain because down in London they've spoken with stretcher bearers that crossed

with the wounded yesterday into Dover. They asked them
were any from up here. They said there were wounded
Manchesters but there were not likely to be any Accringtons
for they were wiped out . . . except for seven.

MAY. How could they know for sure?

SARAH. They were there! They still had the dirt and mess on
their uniforms. And there was a young officer. He said
he wasn't supposed to confirm it . . . but he did. And he was
a big well-spoken young man but he was crying.

EVA. They treat us like children but we'll not behave like
children. D'you believe it now May? I've been thinking and
talking to one or two up the street. There's a general opinion
that we should force them to tell us properly at the Town
Hall. And we should all go there in the morning and make
sure they do. And I mean everybody. Will you two go round
with me and knock on doors?

SARAH. Yes. That's good. Bertha and me'll do all Waterloo
Street if you like . . .

BERTHA. I couldn't . . .

SARAH. You can! We'll get that bloody Mayor stood in front
of us and if he says he doesn't know he can get on his telephone
to wherever and find out! We'll march there! Come on
Bertha. Let's get started.

BERTHA. If only they could be alive!

    SARAH *leads her away.*

EVA. You'll come with us May —

MAY. No!

EVA. D'you still not believe it?

MAY. I believe what I believe.

EVA. Will you let yourself believe that Tom's one of the seven?

MAY. I shall find out myself.

EVA. How? That's what we're going for.

MAY. Marching!

EVA. We're going together, that's all.

MAY. They should make up their own minds . . .

EVA. They will. It's little enough we're asking. We just want to know. For all of us.

MAY. If Tom's hurt . . . if they've hurt him . . . I'll find out. And I'll find out for myself.

EVA goes. MAY stands stock still and after some moments calls softly.

MAY. Tom . . . Tom . . .

Into her imagination comes the sound of guns in a series of faint echoes. The stage darkens. A flare going off in the distance bathes the edge of the stage in white light. It fades. REGGIE runs on.

REGGIE. Did you see it Miss? Did you?

MAY. What?

REGGIE. Lights in the sky. We've seen three from back kitchen up over the moors. I thought it were a zepplin on fire. Mother saw it. Her thinks it's to light the way from France. Thinks it's the Germans burning the moor. That they've killed all our soldiers and they're coming through . . . she's real bad. I'm sent for doctor.

Getting no response from MAY he goes. She stares at the sky.

MAY. Where? Where?

She rushes to the stall and closes the tarpaulin. She crosses forward on the darkened stage looking for lights.

Tom . . . shall I dare to look at you? Are you crawling? Are you breathing?

A louder burst of machine gun fire. She jumps back against the tarpaulin.

Where's those lights? I want to see you. I'm not scared . . . they're the ones who are scared. Afraid to stand on their own!

A flare. CSM RIVERS enters.

RIVERS. That's the spirit, Miss.

MAY. You!

RIVERS. I always admired your spirit.

MAY. Where's Tom?

RIVERS. Near. You're with the Pals.

MAY. Show me Tom.

RIVERS. He'll come to you. You've brought yourself so far. He'll come.

MAY. He's alive!

RIVERS. In my care.

A flare. MAY *cowers.*

Stand up Miss Hassel. Nothing'll reach you here.

MAY. Oh the stench!

RIVERS. A bit ripe. A bit gamey. And Fritz don't help, stirring up the offal.

MAY. Will Tom be here soon?

RIVERS. They all will. He'll report here.

MAY. But they said only seven were left!

RIVERS. Seven? That's a rumour number. There's only five hundred and eighty five dead or wounded . . . and that leaves near a hundred. Not so bad as your West Yorks or Tynesiders.

MAY. Which way are the Germans?

RIVERS. Up there.

MAY. Give me that rifle.

RIVERS. Well you are a Tartar. Could you use it?

MAY. Show me.

RIVERS. I'm honoured, Miss Hassel. But not in anger or hate. That only upsets the aim. Kneel. Thighs braced apart . . . but easy.

He holds the rifle in position. She presses the butt to her shoulder.

Not against the collar bone. Just under it there's a pad of flesh that God provided for the convenience of riflemen. Nurse it to you. Twist your arm in the sling, so. Take the weight.

MAY. It's heavy!

RIVERS. As a lover . . . that being my fancy to say to the men and remind them what comforts them most in the presence of death . . . for fear, like anger and hate, make a bad rifleman. Look along the barrel to the tip of the foresight . . . which it is my whim to call the male . . . for as you see, the back sight is a slit . . . open and ready to receive. Bring the one gently to the other . . . Have they touched?

MAY. Yes.

RIVERS. When I say so take a short breath for the count of two. No longer or you'll begin to waver. Understood?

MAY. Yes.

RIVERS. When you see your target, which I call the object of desire . . .

TOM *enters, shadowy.*

MAY (*sensing him*): There! There!

RIVERS. Make a moment of calm and . . . squeeze the trigger lovingly!

She fires at the shadowy figure. TOM raises his head, as though the shot raised a memory. His face is the face of a corpse.

MAY. Tom!

RIVERS. I said he'd come to you.

MAY. Tom!

RIVERS. Keep away. They spit like toads some of them. He'd tear the inside from your body if he could. Look at his eyes.

MAY. But it's Tom . . .

RIVERS. Don't insult him by putting his name to that! None of

us would want our names put to what we are in the first few
hours of death. All we are then is what we spew up in our last
belch. Blind panic, vengeance, and terror . . . that's all we are
at first. Flying off the battlefield screaming like starlings.
It's all a poor soldier can do to fling himself down on the
earth and cling onto life with his bleeding fingertips till
they've sailed by freezing the skin up his back. But our Tom
was a hero. He saw his good friends die, the old one refusing
God, the young one shot, his head puffed up blue as a
sugar bag as the bullet went through. You went fighting
mad didn't you boy? Waving his rifle at that flock of
ghosts — all shrieking and chirping. Ah . . . he remembers.

MAY. Tom! It's May . . .

TOM *leaps back, snarling.*

RIVERS. Come on boy. This is Miss Hassal. Speak love to him.
Pity him. Tell him he should have a medal. That's what
he wants to hear. He's full of envy that someone else is alive,
d'ye see?

MAY (*to* TOM): I should have loved you . . .

RIVERS. Don't say that. Tell him he died a hero.

MAY. He died a slave!

RIVERS. He died a soldier, with his brothers in arms . . .

MAY. No! He was alone. In the end you're on your own. I told
him time and again. It's hard. It's unbearable. But you've
got to believe it! If only he'd stood up for himself and
not let himself be led . . . then I shouldn't have killed him.

RIVERS. You? Hear that boy? Why the one that did that was
some little pot-bellied Woortenberger . . . some pint-sized
sausage eater, wasn't he boy? Stood up on his parapet
thinking all the Tommies were wiped out . . . then sees
this mad-cap scarecrow ripping his way out of the wire. Bang!
Tom's dead.

TOM *has begun to grin at the memory.*

TOM. We exchanged our skills. No money was involved . . .

MAY. Slave! If you hadn't died like one you'd have lived like
one. Oh this stench! This stink!

RIVERS. Come on Hackford. Up!

MAY. Your words . . . your dreams . . . your promised lands . . . your living for others . . . none of it would have saved you!

RIVERS. Get fell in!

MAY. You'd have groused and grumbled about your dunderheads and numbskulls . . . but all the same when they opened their cage to you you'd have walked right in and locked the door. They'd have taken everything and all the love in the world would have made no difference.

RIVERS. Up with the others on the road. Move!

MAY. No! I want you to condemn me . . .

She reaches out her hands to TOM.

I sat there . . . and I thought it would be better if you didn't come back.

TOM *stares at her hands. A memory of life stirs in him. He reaches out and gently touches them.* MAY *feels the cold strike through her.*

RIVERS. Get on parade Hackford! Fall in you happy warriors! Get fell in the Pals! Move yourselves you glorious dead!

We hear the parade. Marching begins. MAY, *staring in horror at her hands, retreats to the stall and sits. Lights fade to blackout.*

Scene Eight

Lights come up on MAY *sitting by the stall.* REGGIE *enters. He pauses.* MAY *doesn't look up.*

REGGIE. Shall I take covers back, miss?

She nods. He begins to tie the sheets back.

Her's more settled now. Mother.

MAY. Oh is she? Good.

REGGIE. They say rest. Just rest. Sorry I didn't come to unpack last night Miss. Shall I get the onions?

He waits for a reply but gets none.
Enter EVA *with a suitcase and more or less the same*

belongings she came with at the beginning of the play.
REGGIE *looks from one to the other.*

EVA. I wasn't sure you'd got my address written down anywhere so I've left it propped up on the mantel shelf.

REGGIE. Shall I get the onions?

EVA *nods. He goes.*

EVA. He can do the stall on his own now. You don't have to sit out here.

MAY. It's funny . . . I've been staring at the backs of my hands and they look very peculiar. Shiny and a bit shrivelled. But then I can't remember when I last looked at them properly. Will your sister want you there long?

EVA. Yes. I've told you. She's at her wits' end. They can scarcely do much at all for themselves. Father's quite incapable.

MAY. I need you to put me right. You seem to know instinctively. You were right about going to Town Hall, weren't you? And the Mayor took it very well . . . sending to the War Office to find out . . . Oh . . . I had such a beautiful letter from Tom's aunt in Salford. (*Puzzled.*) Did I . . . show it you?

EVA. Yes. May, I'm going.

MAY. Shall we ask Reggie to get the cart and wheel your things to the stop?

EVA. It's all right. Sarah and Bertha are waiting to walk along with me.

MAY. Oh yes. I won't come then.

EVA. May, you're welcome to come!

MAY. No, I don't think I will. But I would like you to do one little thing for me. It was just something in the paper yesterday. That man who writes the poems . . . I expect you saw it.

EVA. Yes.

MAY (*getting the paper from the stall*): You read things so well. Would you?

EVA. Oh May . . . don't ask me . . .

MAY. Please. I'd like to hear it read.

> EVA *takes the paper reluctantly.*

EVA.
> 'There are tear-dimmed eyes in the town today,
> There are lips to be no more kissed . . .'

> REGGIE *enters with the basket.* MAY *motions him to stand still.*

MAY. Just a moment, Reggie.

> *The sight of the two of them waiting for her to continue increases* EVA's *anger with the situation.*

EVA.
> 'There are bosoms that swell with an aching heart
> When they think of their dear ones missed.
> But time will . . .' (*Breaks off.*) I don't know this word. I don't know it.

> *But* MAY *still waits patiently.* EVA *is forced to continue.*

> 'But time will . . .' something . . .

MAY. 'Assauge . . .'

EVA.
> . . . their heartfelt grief
> Of their sons they will proudly tell
> How in gallant charge in the world wide war
> As Pals they fought and fell.'

> *She hands back the paper to* MAY *with:*

> It doesn't say what I feel. Makes me angry.

MAY. Well you can't put everything in one poem.

EVA. Bye May. Bye Reggie.

> EVA *goes.* REGGIE *puts the basket on the stall.*

MAY. Oh those are good onions. You have done well. I shall have to start paying you more.

> *Bugle band.*

MADE AND PRINTED IN GREAT BRITAIN BY
LATIMER TREND & COMPANY LTD, PLYMOUTH
MADE IN ENGLAND